JUMPSTART! FRENCH AND GERMAN

ENGAGING ACTIVITIES FOR AGES 7–12

Catherine Watts and Hilary Phillips

First published 2014
by Routledge
2 Park Square, Milton Park, Abingdon, Oxon OX14 4RN

and by Routledge
711 Third Avenue, New York, NY 10017

Routledge is an imprint of the Taylor & Francis Group, an informa business

© 2014 Catherine Watts and Hilary Phillips

British Library Cataloguing in Publication Data
A catalogue record for this book is available from the British Library

Library of Congress Cataloging in Publication Data
Watts, Catherine.
Jumpstart! French and German : engaging activities for ages 7–12 / Catherine Watts, Hilary Phillips.
pages cm. — (Jumpstart!)
1. Language and languages—Study and teaching (Secondary)
2. French language—Study and teaching (Secondary) 3. German language—Study and teaching (Secondary) 4. Interdisciplinary approach in education. I. Phillips, Hilary. II. Title.
P53.W38 2014
372.65′31044—dc23
2013034330

ISBN: 978-0-415-85695-9 (pbk)
ISBN: 978-1-315-81483-4 (ebk)

Typeset in Palatino and Scala San
by FiSH Books Ltd, Enfield

Printed and bound in Great Britain by
TJ International Ltd, Padstow, Cornwall

JUMPSTART!
FRENCH AND GERMAN

Jumpstart! French and German presents a collection of simple to use, multi-sensory games and activities that will jumpstart students' understanding of modern languages into action. If you are one of the thousands of teachers looking for a range of practical and fun ideas to teach languages engagingly, then this is the perfect book for you.

The book opens with a range of innovative ideas to help you set the scene in your language classroom. These are followed by a feast of short and simple activities designed to help you make quick starts with your students and hold their attention. The focus throughout is on communicative action, bringing languages alive, with all activities presented in two languages: French and German. Specifically written to help teachers work within the guidelines of the new curriculum, activities in the book will help pupils to:

- listen to, respond to and understand key elements of the target language
- speak in phrases and sentences with appropriate pronunciation
- express and communicate simple ideas with clarity
- write phrases and short sentences
- develop an understanding of basic grammar
- learn songs and simple poems in the language studied
- engage in active learning through a range of varied activities.

Jumpstart! French and German celebrates the joys of language and will help you to find just the right words or phrases to express what you want to say.

Catherine Watts is currently Director of the Routes into Languages South consortium and is Principal Lecturer in English Language and German within the Faculty of Arts and Humanities as well as contributing to the EdD, PGCE and MA in Education at the University of Brighton, UK.

Hilary Phillips has been a primary class teacher for over 20 years. She was also Lead Teacher for Primary Languages in Brighton and Hove and has co-presented at several local and national conferences.

Also available

Jumpstart! Literacy
Key Stage 2/3 Literacy Games
Pie Corbett
978-1-84312-102-6

Jumpstart! Numeracy
Maths Activities and Games for Ages 5–14
John Taylor
978-1-84312-264-2

Jumpstart! ICT
ICT Activities and Games for Ages 7–14
John Taylor
978-1-84312-465-8

Jumpstart! Creativity
Games and Activities for Ages 7–14
Steve Bowkett
978-0-415-43273-3

To our students and colleagues: past, present and future.

CW and HP

Contents

Contents

Vocabulary Topics

Simple greetings 1
Taking the register
Sporting vocabulary
Newsletter language
Room labels
Welcome
Polite phrases 1
Months of the year
Introductory questions
School subjects
Describing people/animals
Counting/colour rhyme
Points of the compass/weather
Growing vegetables and flowers
Playground signs
Expressing negatives
Odd/even numbers
Take two steps
Points of the compass/locations
Positions
Body parts 1
Body parts 2
Action verbs 1
Action verbs 2
Clock times
Show me a...
Useful phrases
Polite phrases 2
Clothes 1
Hot potatoes
Beginnings

Asking questions 1
I'm ill
Prices and items
Basic moves
Touch colours...
Commands
Mister Monster / Wolf
Days of the week
Quantities
The post
Fruit Salad
Polite phrases 3
Adjective animals
Asking questions 2
Traffic lights
Directions
Clothes 2
Describing a monster
Aquaria / sealife
Describing emotions
Simple greetings 2
Describing clothes
Recipes
Transport
Rain forest
Christmas
Fruit
Farm animals
Food
Daily routines 1
Weather / seasons
Classroom instructions
Body parts 3
Reverse counting
Actions
Daily routines 2
Colours
Animals
Describing people

Clothes to wear
Cooking pancakes
Animals and actions
Menus
Food
Likes and dislikes
Shopping
Adjectives
Celebrations
Writing an e-mail
Writing a postcard
Weather 1
Writing a poem
Animal habitats
Stationery items
Weather 2
Simon Says...
Tongue twisters
Snow rhyme
Weekdays rhyme
Describing objects
Farewell routines

List of Figures

Acknowledgements

The authors and publishers would like to thank the following people for their help with both the text and the artwork in *Jumpstart! French and German*. Every effort has been made to contact copyright holders for their permission to reprint material in this book. The publishers would be grateful to hear from any copyright holder who is not here acknowledged and will undertake to rectify any errors or omissions in future editions of this book.

TEXT

Grateful thanks are due to Astrid Masson (Lewes Old Grammar School) and Sandrine Stringer (Upper Beeding Primary School) for helping us with the translations and final proof-reading.

ARTWORK

We are most grateful to **b small publishing ltd** for allowing us to design some of the artwork (© b small publishing ltd.) in Chapter 5 using their stencils. Specific publications we have targeted are all by Clare Beaton: *Farm animals; Under the sea; Make your own rainforest; Wild animals; Paper dolls; Cars and trucks*. These delightful books and stencils are very reasonably priced and available through www.bsmall.co.uk.

We are also grateful to Nicola Goodland for the fruit illustrations in Chapter 5 and some of the Christmas illustrations in the same chapter, as well as the illustrations of *The Three Little Pigs* in Chapter 7. Our thanks are also due to Alex Chown for some of the Christmas illustrations in Chapter 5 too.

Introduction

Why teach young children a foreign language? Most language experts agree that there is a highly efficient 'window of opportunity' for young learners to absorb a new language efficiently. In other words: the younger the better in terms of learning a new language! It is certainly easier for young children to absorb a new language without the selfconsciousness and embarrassment of older learners. They are keen and fresh, full of curiosity about new ideas, ready to experiment, open to new experiences and eager to find out about how other people live. They love getting their tongues around strange new sounds, even those that do not feature in their mother tongue. They are in one of the most productive learning phases of their lives and they lap up the sheer fun of the experience.

In this book we aim to encourage you to motivate your class to become keen language learners through a wide range of exciting activities and games. You may be excited or daunted at the prospect ahead; perhaps you feel that your own experience of language learning was off-putting or that your knowledge is limited or rusty. Well, you have a welcome surprise ahead; children love languages and with the right primary-based methodology and structure, they make great progress. Bear in mind that you are not preparing them for an exam, but rather an introduction. Your motto should be: *Do a lot with a little*. Take small steps, practise the same information in many different ways, experiment with new ideas and enjoy the whole experience. As a primary teacher, you will already have routines set up; use the strategies and games that make up a normal day in a primary classroom and slip in a foreign language naturally. If you are lucky enough to have Reception or Early Years classes in your school, walk around their classrooms and remind yourself of how young children start to learn. Many of the skills can be reproduced for a new language.

The materials in *Jumpstart! French and German* seek to motivate and inspire: all are replicable/adaptable and all stem from actual classroom experience. We hope they will inspire your teaching, motivate your students and add further possibilities to your foreign language classrooms and beyond to be enjoyed by everyone. If you are a teacher in the UK, you will find an excellent support in the National Framework for Primary Languages, which contains a wealth of expert guidance to help you to set up good practice and to ensure progression. It is easy to read, full of little tips and suggestions for activities and sets out clearly the stages which children need to follow throughout their early years of language learning. It can be accessed through www.primarylanguages.org.

Jumpstart! French and German contains a wealth of lively, flexible and engaging materials across ten chapters which can be dipped into as and when required, rather than being worked through in chronological order. There are: ideas to help you set up your classroom, or even your school, ready to welcome a foreign language; tips for early reading and writing activities; simple craft plans, songs to sing and games to consolidate learning. If time is short, there are quick fillers to fit those impromptu gaps in a busy day and to send your class home with a new language ringing in their ears. To make it easy, all the relevant basic French and German is set out to help you to go straight ahead.

Have fun!   **Viel Spass!**   **Amusez-vous bien**

CHAPTER 1
Setting the Scene

This chapter has two separate aims which will help you to start up or encourage further language learning in your school. First, there are tried and tested ways to slip languages seamlessly into the current school day in your class or even throughout the whole school. If you are the languages co-ordinator, or just a keen teacher, you could pioneer these methods and help more reluctant colleagues to follow your example. With a little practice, it should be possible to hear some basic language exchanges, songs and chanting carried out in the new language in each classroom every morning and afternoon. Remember that your motto will be: *Do a lot with a little;* so you will be starting with simple vocabulary repeated in many different ways over a school week.

Second, there are suggestions to help you to set up your school and classroom space as a vibrant bilingual area in order to stimulate language learning and to slot language into other areas of the curriculum. First impressions certainly count and you can sense the atmosphere of a school just walking down the corridor and peering into classrooms. This could be a golden opportunity for you to promote a new language and to conjure up the lure and exoticism of another way of life or country. In primary schools, 'display' is a great tool to intrigue, stimulate, captivate children's attention and imagination and celebrate their achievements. Whether you have at your disposal just a small corner of a classroom, a single display board in a corridor or even a complete classroom, this is your chance to stimulate the children in your class (and others), provide food for thought and show off their achievements. If you work in a school with young children (ages four to six), pop into their classrooms and remind yourself of how their teachers immerse children in the new world of the written word, and then copy some of their ideas.

ADDING LANGUAGE TO EXISTING CLASSROOM ROUTINES

The simplest way to start languages resounding around your school on a daily basis is to use the target language in classroom exchanges which are part of the normal primary school day. Examples include: morning greetings; taking the dinner register; counting how many children are away and so on. Try to spread the idea around the whole school by practising first in an assembly so that all the teaching staff and children alike know what is expected and feel comfortable. Children soon get used to repeating a formal greeting and response in the target language such as:

English
Good morning. How are you? I'm fine thanks.

French
Bonjour les enfants. Bonjour Monsieur/Madame.
Comment ça va ? Ça va bien, merci.

German
Guten Morgen. Wie geht's? Gut, danke.

Registers
The next step is to call out the class register in the same way, addressing each child in turn and expecting each one to respond. By adding on just a few extra words, children can answer the dinner register. Before going to lunch, a friendly way to start lunchtime would be to wish the class a good meal (and on another occasion, discuss why we don't have such a phrase in our own language!) and to expect them to repeat the phrase to you.

English
School dinner or packed lunch, Joshua?
School dinner please, Madame.
Enjoy your meal!

French
La cantine ou les sandwiches, Joshua?
La cantine s'il vous plaît, Madame.
Bon appétit !

German
Die Kantine oder belegte Brote?
Die Kantine bitte, Frau X.
Guten Appetit!

Counting activities
Counting can be slipped into many daily activities: count the number of children having school dinner or packed lunch each day by asking them to stand up and then you all count along the line. Look for any chance to use numbers when you are lining up for assembly or games or waiting for children to get changed. Count the number of people on the green table, the number of children who are absent that day, anyone with a birthday in July, how many children are left handed etc.

Using assembly time
In assembly, when the whole school is together, a great start could be made to the occasion with the now familiar language greeting from a teacher, *Hello children!*, and the response from all the children. As part of the assembly, teach a new classroom instruction for the whole school and reinforce it in the corridors and playground, as well as in each classroom. Add the instructions to a prominent poster in each classroom and play games with them, trying to catch the children out. Start with easy ones which could lend themselves to a game such as *sit down and stand up*. The whole school could gradually adopt instructions such as: *get into a line; listen; look* (see Appendix 2 for useful classroom language in French and German).

Getting changed
While your class gets changed for physical education, sing a favourite language song from Chapter 6, 'Using Songs', or from your favourite commercial CD, and practise some suitable language ready for your lesson.

3

English
Come on the blues / reds / yellows / greens!
The blues have won!
You (one person) have won. You (more than one person)
have won!

French
Allez les bleus / les rouges / les jaunes / les verts !
Les bleus ont gagné !
Tu as gagné. Vous avez gagné !

German
Los die Blauen, die Roten, die Gelben, die Grünen!
Die Blauen haben gewonnen!
Du hast gewonnen! Ihr habt gewonnen!

Song assembly

If you have a regular song assembly when all teachers are present, introduce a new, simple song for everyone to learn each week. You could use one of the examples in Chapter 6, 'Using Songs', as a starting point and encourage all teachers to practise singing with their classes during the week in spare moments. This is an ideal opportunity to train both staff and students at the same time and to make sure that everyone knows how to pronounce key vocabulary.

Christmas

Try to squeeze a language song into a Christmas assembly. It could be the well-known traditional French song *Vive le vent* to the tune of *Jingle Bells* (available on many commercial CDs and see also page 150 in Chapter 7, 'Exploring Stories'); or you could make up your own by adapting a few Christmas phrases. For example, to the tune of *We Wish You a Merry Christmas*, you could sing:

Bonne Année et Joyeux Noël x 3
Bonne Année à vous !

Phrase of the week

Choose a phrase of the week for the whole school to learn and practise in the classroom. Introduce the phrase in the first school assembly of the week when all pupils and teachers are present. Make life easier for less confident teachers by preparing laminated flashcards of the phrase of the week to be put up in each classroom. Put classroom instruction words up on the central server for everyone to access (see Appendix 2 for some suggestions).

If you have a newsletter which goes home each week, have a section to highlight the phrase and its meaning to encourage families to learn together. Many parents and carers often comment to schools that they would like to be more involved in learning a new language alongside their child and a newsletter presents an ideal opportunity. Keep the language simple and you are more likely to achieve good participation. Here are some examples you could use:

Week One	**English:**	Good morning Miss X; Good morning Mr X.
	French:	Bonjour Madame ; Bonjour Monsieur.
	German:	Guten Morgen Frau X; Guten Morgen Herr X.
Week Two	**English:**	How are you? I'm fine.
	French:	Comment ça va ? Ça va bien !
	German:	Wie geht's? Gut danke!
Week Three	**English:**	My name is...
	French:	Je m'appelle...
	German:	Ich heiße...
Week Four	**English:**	Stand up; Sit down.
	French:	Levez-vous; Asseyez-vous.
	German:	Steht auf; Setzt euch.
Week Five	**English:**	Listen carefully.
	French:	Écoutez bien.
	German:	Hört gut zu.

HOW TO TURN YOUR SCHOOL INTO A BILINGUAL AREA

In the school corridors or entrance lobby

Make an impression at the door by putting up a large colourful language poster showing a few simple phrases, such as:

English
Hello! How are you; Do you speak French/German?
French/German is great!

French
Bonjour ! Comment ça va ? Parlez-vous français/allemand ?
Le français/l'allemand, c'est fantastique !

German
Guten Morgen! Wie geht's? Sprechen Sie
Französisch/Deutsch? Französisch/Deutsch ist toll!

Every school has a welcome sign to greet visitors at the entrance. This could be developed into a collection of speech bubble greetings of all the languages spoken by children in the school community. Designing speech bubbles written by the children themselves is considered in Chapter 9, 'Starting to Write'.

If you're assembling a display board in a school corridor, liven it up with a colourful foreign language border to signpost that this is a different sort of display. There are a range of borders available online (for example www.linguascope.com) showing days of the week, colours, speech bubbles, introductory phrases. Children are drawn to the captions and like to spot the phrase they recognise as they walk past.

Stringing up bunting with little pennants of multi-national flags is a simple and cheap transformation to make. They are available from various online suppliers (for example www.little-linguist.co.uk) and can be limited to one country's flag or a variety. Larger flags are also easy to find, perhaps to place near the school entrance.

Room labels

Create or buy labels for the rooms in the school, including a picture of the room and its name in the target language. You could ask the class to make their own pictures and labels, laminate them and stick them up outside the rooms. If this goes well, label parts of the classroom too, using a bilingual dictionary to find the correct vocabulary.

English	French	German
classroom	la salle de classe	das Klassenzimmer
cloakroom	le vestiaire	die Garderobe
canteen	la cantine	die Kantine
computer suite	la salle d'informatique	das Computerzimmer
corridor	le couloir	der Flur
library	la bibliothèque	die Bibliothek
toilets	les toilettes	die Toiletten

The head master's/headmistress's office is *le bureau du Directeur/ de la Directrice* in French and *das Direktorbüro/ das Direktorinbüro* in German.

Welcome

Each class could design a welcome sign and place it outside the door.

French: Bienvenue à notre classe !

German: Herzlich Willkommen in unserem Klassenzimmer!

Language posters
Students could design posters about how great/useful languages are. Laminate them and place them in the corridors around the school.

Teacher models
Use your colleagues as language speaking role models around the school. Greet each other appropriately in the target language when you meet each other in public areas such as corridors. Take photos of them and place appropriate speech bubbles in the new language of what they might say! A sporty teacher might say, for example, *I like playing football,* whilst another might say *I can read a menu and order food when I'm on holiday.* Attach the speech bubbles to the photos and place them on the walls around the school.

In the classroom
Look at your classroom in a completely new way. With any sign or display you usually put up, think of adding a little foreign language to it. If you have table groups for maths, literacy or science, the subject names could have a subtitle. The equipment or fittings in your room could be labelled, for example: *the window; the door; the bookcase.* Colour groups or talk partners for activities could be renamed. Days of the week could be written as a colourful list alongside their English equivalents. Even coat pegs could have a picture and a caption in the new language!

Everyday vocabulary displays
Put up prominently a large poster of a lunchbox and school dinner food display alongside the relevant vocabulary so that children can answer the dinner register in another language each morning.

In a handy place where everyone can see, put on the wall lots of polite phrases in the foreign language to encourage the class to use them in everyday conversation. Below are some examples. Give team points to tables which take these up regularly.

English	French	German
Good morning	Bonjour	Guten Morgen
Good afternoon	Bonjour	Guten Tag
Enjoy your meal!	Bon appétit !	Guten Appetit!
Hi!	Salut !	Hallo!
Goodbye	Au revoir	Auf Wiedersehen
please	s'il vous plaît	bitte
thank you	merci	danke
yes	oui	ja
no	non	nein
I'd like a...	je voudrais un(e)...	Ich möchte ein/eine/einen...

Birthdays
Create a display based on the usual birthday posters containing months of the year labelled in the foreign language. Add the names of the children to the appropriate month as their birthday comes up. Older children could write their birthday dates and names to be clipped with pegs onto a washing line strung across the room.

English	French	German
January	janvier	Januar
February	février	Februar
March	mars	März
April	avril	April
May	mai	Mai

June	juin	Juni
July	juillet	Juli
August	août	August
September	septembre	September
October	octobre	Oktober
November	novembre	November
December	décembre	Dezember

What do you know?
Make a picture card display posing the question *How many of these do you know?* in English, with a realistic number of words and pictures from the current topic spaced around the pictures. Encourage children to check their running total after every language lesson.

Hoops
Don't forget about the ceiling! You can use it to suspend hoops from which you can hang flashcards of the questions and answers from your current topic. Back-to-back materials avoid blank backs and maximise ceiling space.

Song words
Put up the words of any new song you've been learning so that children can practise while they line up or get dressed for physical education.

Our word collections
Encourage children to bring back phrases they have seen on their own travels in other countries, write them up and investigate what they might mean. This is a good way to immerse them in other languages and encourage curiosity about the similarities and differences between languages.

Don't do this!
Children enjoy the idea of creating their own rules and might

appreciate the idea of forbidding something in their classroom. Use the phrase *It is forbidden to...* and add some sensible and not so sensible verbs to make a commanding display for the wall.

English
It is forbidden to sing/eat/drink/sleep/dance/smile... in this classroom!

French
Il est défendu de chanter/manger/boire/dormir/danser/sourire... dans cette salle de classe !

German
Es ist verboten zu singen/essen/trinken/schlafen/tanzen/lächeln... in diesem Klassenzimmer!

Friends around the world
If you have a link with another school in a foreign country, put up photos of these new friends and add speech bubbles with details of their lives, for example *for breakfast I eat... / in my spare time I like....* Explore differences and similarities with the children in your own class.

LANGUAGE WORK DISPLAYS

Posters of the most frequently taught topics are easy to locate on line (for example, www.lajolieronde.co.uk). A3-size greetings, classroom equipment, numbers and colours can form the starting point of an open-ended display to which you can add children's written work at a later date (see also Chapter 9, 'Starting to Write').

This is me
Take a photo of each child or ask them to draw a self-portrait to which they add a speech bubble saying *hello*, their name, age and any other information suitable to their level of target language

11

learning, for example, their favourite colour. These look good hanging from ceiling hoops or on the wall as an introduction to the class at the beginning of the school year. Stick two sides together if you hang them from the ceiling, so there are no blank sides.

Useful language

As part of your language lesson, ask the class to help to make eye-catching displays for your boards labelled in the new language. Simple ones could include colours, with the children colouring in a particular shape, such as a fish or a rainbow, and labelling the coloured area(s) with the correct colour name. Number words can be displayed inside balloons in a bunch with a number word attached. Pictures of classroom equipment with the name attached are also effective, for example, *pen*, *ruler* and so on.

Mix and match

Make a big display containing a mix-and-match game with lots of introductory questions:

English	French	German
What's your name?	Comment tu t'appelles ?	Wie heißt du?
How are you?	Ça va ?	Wie geht's?
What's the time?	Quelle heure est-il ?	Wie spät ist es?
How old are you?	Quel âge as-tu ?	Wie alt bist du?

Add a variety of answers jumbled up on the board and invite children to sort them as a quiz posted in a letter box. Alternatively, you could spend five minutes once a week rearranging the questions and their answers in the correct formation and then scrambling them again to see if they can improve by the following week.

School life

At the start of the school term make a welcoming and positive display about school life and subjects, for example:

English	French	German
I'm good at history	Je suis fort en histoire	Ich bin gut in Geschichte
I love maths	J'aime les maths	Ich liebe Mathe
I prefer geography	Je préfère la géographie	Ich bevorzuge Geographie

Families

For Mothers' Day and other family celebrations, display picture poems in the target language. For example, children draw a picture of their mother in the centre and add words around to describe her in the foreign language such as:

English	French	German
she is...	elle est...	sie ist...
happy/ kind/ beautiful	heureuse/ gentille/ belle	glücklich/ freundlich/ schön

Animal bubbles

For an animal topic, children draw a picture of an animal of their choice in the centre with simple words coming from the speech bubble such as:

English	French	German
I am an elephant	je suis un éléphant	Ich bin ein Elefant
and I am big / grey / fierce	et je suis grand / gris / féroce	und ich bin groß / grau / wild

CULTURAL INTEREST DISPLAYS

Create a display to draw attention to cultural differences which could be captioned in English as well as the foreign language. You could take breakfast food and drink, for example, with questions about children in another country such as *What do German children have for breakfast? What do French children have for school lunch?* This could link to information obtained from your partner school (see Chapter 9, 'Starting to Write').

Market stalls
Make up the start of a large market or specialist food shop display on a table top where children could draw or make typical food for sale and label it with a price. You could add the times and days of the week when the market or shop is open and a bold welcome sign.

Investigate any unusual festivals or special customs in the term ahead such as Bastille Day in France (July 14th) or St Martin's Day in Germany (November 2nd). Explore the topic together and put up information from the internet with an explanation of what goes on and photos. If possible, have a mini-celebration in class and add class pictures to the display. There are some good ideas about celebrating special days in other countries in Part Three of *Living Languages: An Integrated Approach to Teaching Foreign Languages in Primary Schools* (Watts, Forder and Phillips, 2013).

Planning a trip
Put up a big map of the country you are studying, label the capital city and main cities and investigate a journey to the capital.

Plan your journey there, what you might see, eat etc. For home-work, ask the children to write a diary entry (in English) of a day in the capital or a speech bubble (in the foreign language) of a conversation they might have and add these to the board.

USING OTHER PEOPLE AROUND YOU

Don't forget to look around and ask for help and support from parents/carers/school staff etc. if any speak the language you are trying to teach. Most people are only too happy to visit classrooms, assemblies and so on to help with pronunciation or lead small-group work.

PLAYGROUND CLAPPING GAMES

Playgrounds are full of children using familiar rhymes and chants in clapping games either in pairs or groups. With a little effort it is possible to have a whole year group (or even more!) clapping chants in another language and teaching each other new ones. Why not spend a little lesson time one week putting together chants in the new language which can be used outside at play-time? It is easy to try, costs nothing and catches on quickly. The main requirements are that the language should be:

- simple to understand
- easy to remember
- repetitive but not rhyming
- catchy to fit a clapping rhythm.

If you want this to start with Year Three children aged around eight, familiar vocabulary such as numbers, colours and greetings will work well. Older children could use compass directions, weather expressions, seasons, family members, body parts, animals and their habitats to construct their own rhymes. A typi-cal early rhyme would be:

English	French	German
one, two, three	un, deux, trois	eins, zwei, drei
red, blue, yellow	rouge, bleu, jaune	rot, blau, gelb
one, two, three	un, deux, trois	eins, zwei, drei
white, green, black	blanc, vert, noir	weiß, grün, schwarz
GOODBYE!!	AU REVOIR !!	AUF WIEDERSEHEN!!

These words can fit into the 'Cross hands and spin around' concept of many games.

A more advanced group might construct:

English	French	German
In the north it's sunny	Au Nord il y a du soleil	Im Norden ist es sonnig
In the south it's windy	Au Sud il y a du vent	Im Süden ist es windig
In the east it's stormy	A l'Est il y a un orage	Im Osten ist es stürmisch
In the west it's snowing!	A l'Ouest il neige !	Im Westen schneit es!

Each rhyme can end with a count downwards, such as:

English: 5, 4, 3, 2, 1, ZERO!

French: Cinq, quatre, trois, deux, un, ZERO !

German: fünf, vier, drei, zwei, eins, NULL!

This can fit in with the topics worked in lessons but end with a turn, triumphant star jump or any other funny flourish – as well as a loud shout on ZERO of course!

Further steps
- Everyone writes up their rhyme to make a class book.
- One class pairs up with a different class and teaches them their rhymes.
- Post up a new rhyme each day in the playground for everyone to practise.
- Have a long chain of people clapping out rhymes on each other's backs.
- Perform one in assembly for the whole school to learn.

EXPLORING THE SCHOOL GROUNDS

Beyond the actual school buildings, there are numerous possibilities for language learning and practice, depending on how much outdoor space you have. You may be lucky enough to have your own vegetable/flower patch, in which case why not label some of the plants in the target language? Here are some ideas for easy-to-grow items:

English	French	German
beans	les haricots	die Bohnen
tomatoes	les tomates	die Tomaten
radishes	les radis	die Radieschen
onions	les oignons	die Zwiebeln
sunflowers	les tournesols	die Sonnenblumen
pumpkins	les citrouilles	die Kürbisse
herbs	les herbes	die Kräuter

Even if you don't have a vegetable patch, you can still display key words and important messages around the grounds. If you laminate the signs they will have a longer life. Here are two examples which will get people talking at least. On a special tree for example you could hang:

English: I am old: please don't climb in my branches!

French: Je suis vieux : s'il vous plaît ne pas monter dans mes branches !

German: Ich bin alt: bitte nicht in meinen Ästen klettern!

In the scooter park you could say:

English: We don't like falling over: please park us properly!

French: Nous n'aimons pas tomber : s'il vous plaît garez-nous correctement!

German: Wir möchten nicht umfallen: bitte parken Sie uns richtig!

YOURSELF

Last, but by no means least, don't forget yourself as a resource! Your abilities to mime, use gestures, count on your fingers, use facial expressions and generally bring the target language to life are absolutely crucial to the success of your foreign language lessons. When you ask children to guess what you are saying as you silently mouth vocabulary items, you are encouraging them to focus hard on what you are doing; when you ask them to guess by your action what the weather is like for example, language learning becomes a game and in itself motivating; when you mime what you want to say, you are helping your children gain a life skill as communication is not about words alone. You yourself are the inspiration in the classroom and the language learning model!

CHAPTER 2
Using Flashcards

The recommended sequence for teaching new vocabulary is to develop listening skills first, starting with listening to new words and sound patterns perhaps in the form of simple rhymes, stories and songs and then responding with a gesture. The next stage involves repeating words and sounds as an echo of the teacher or native speaker on a CD etc. and beginning to listen out for specific examples of those words and sounds. After lots of practice, the written word is then introduced and matched up with the spoken word so that children have tuned in to the distinctive sounds of a language and are not put off by the disconcerting spelling in front of them. In the early stages of language learning, oracy (in the form of listening and speaking) is the key skill to develop and that is why you will need a vast array of flashcard activities to convey meaning and a broad selection of games to practise new language.

You will need to practise new vocabulary over and over again in as many different ways as possible for children to learn and then to revise at intervals to keep it fresh in their minds. Don't under-estimate how much practice they will need, so aim to keep it lively, varied and fun. Dip into these suggestions; you will soon discover your own favourites. Most of these are on the basis of 'you say, they repeat...'.

Most teachers introduce vocabulary using flashcards to set the scene for new rhymes and songs. You may want to start with picture flashcards only and add separate text cards at the next stage; as a bonus, a matching up game of text and pictures is often a good starter to revise vocabulary from the previous lesson. Some people use flashcards with text on them from the start and just draw attention to the text at the appropriate stage.

You could make your own bright and bold A4 flashcards by finding suitable coloured photos online, adding text as large as possible and laminating them. If you prefer, you can buy suitable A4 cards from many of the languages resources suppliers (for example: www.little-linguist.co.uk; www.language-stickers.co.uk; www.linguascope.co.uk; www.eslkidstuff.com / flashcards.htm; www.primaryclassroom resources.co.uk) on a variety of topics such as animals, the weather, clothes, food etc.

FLASHCARD GAMES

Encourage children just to listen to new words the first time and repeat them in their head or under their breath just to get a feel for the language. Then play some games during which they echo your words.

Listen and repeat games: Calling Out
Vary the volume of your voice by saying the new words in a whisper, a bit louder and, when they least expect it, a shout. Children love this idea, as they rarely have a genuine excuse for shouting!

Many Faces
Give your face an expression and say the word in the appropriate voice, for example: happy; sad; angry; surprised; scared; timid; crying; romantic; singing on two notes, first going up and then down.

Point It Out
Point to the one I'm saying! The children have to repeat what you say too. Although this seems rather obvious, it's a good way of linking the written and spoken word and enables you to see who needs more help.

Syllables Clap
Call out the syllables and clap them on your knees, or beat three fingers on the palm of your hand or use open hands in the air.

Wave Your Arms
Stand up and call out the syllables in the new word, moving your arms in the air, moving your arms to one side and then the other, touching your shoulders, hips etc.

Sing Up
Sing the word or phrase repeatedly to a familiar tune such as *London's burning*. Point to the card you are going to sing and ask your class to join in with you or as an echo.

Mouth It
Mouth the word silently with exaggerated lips. The children guess which word you are saying.

Picture Fans
All these introductory games could be continued with the use of mini-hand-held picture fans of the appropriate vocabulary so that children can play the same games with a partner (see Chapter 5, 'Being Creative', for details on making fans).

MEMORY GAMES

Quick Flash
Tantalise your class with a quick flashcard of the word so they only catch a glimpse. They call out from memory, using the target language of course!

Slow Reveal
Show just one tiny corner of the card and gradually reveal more, or hide one in an envelope and do the same. Again, the children call the word out when they think they recognise it.

Hide It
Hide a flashcard behind your back and ask the class to guess which it is.

Guess My Choice
Place a series of perhaps ten cards on the board. Without looking

at the cards, say the names of a random selection of five of them, one after the other. Children have to try to remember which ones you've said in the right order.

What's Missing?

Place a series of cards on the board and chant the words together. Ask children to close their eyes while you remove one. What's missing? When they are all back on the board read them aloud again.

Feely Bag

Put a selection of items to match the flashcards in a feely bag, for example, puppets to match animal cards, plastic food, classroom equipment such as rulers or pencils. Count aloud up to ten, twenty or whatever is appropriate as you pass the bag around the class until the last number is up. The child with the bag opens it and has to say the name of the item they can feel or that they extract from the bag. With the food items, the children could say whether or not they like/dislike them.

MORE COMPLICATED GAMES

The following flashcard games are more complicated, but once everyone has got the idea, invite a volunteer to come out and have a go, or ask the children to play in pairs or a threesome.

Is It This Or Is It That?

For example, is it a pear or an apple? The children say which it is.

Only If I'm Right

Say the name of the card, sometimes correctly, sometimes the wrong word. The children have to listen carefully and only repeat it if it's the correct one.

Thumbs Up

Practise the usual process of 'you point to a picture card, they say the phrase', but whenever you say a particular word such as *monkey*, the children have to put their thumbs up in the air. This encourages good listening if you slip the *monkey* in quite often. You could choose any action such as clap hands once, stand up or stamp your feet, to go with any random word of your choice.

Spot the Phoneme
From an early stage, it is important to identify sounds and match up phonemes just as we do in literacy lessons from reception class onwards. Put up a series of cards showing the written word with some matching sounds, such as in French the letters *oi* making the sound *wha*. They include *moi, toi, fois, bois, croissant*. In German you could have for example *zwei, drei, mein, Stein*, with the *ei* making the *i* sound (as in the English *fine*). Practise the sound in as many ways as you can think, match up the words with the same sound and build up a collection of words on a poster in the classroom.

Mimes
Decide on a mime for the new word. Practise together, then play the game where you say the word and the children mime the action; next, you mime the action and they say the word. Always do it this way round so that they get as much practice as possible hearing the new vocabulary.

Match Mimes
Once the children have got used to the miming game above, try this more complicated version. You do a mime and show a picture or a written text card. If they are correctly matched, children say the word involved. If not, they remain silent.

Sorting
Arrange the new vocabulary into alphabetical order. Invite volunteers to come up to hold a card and place it in dictionary order using the initial letter, then the second and third etc.

Consonant/Vowel Game
Check that everyone remembers which letters are vowels and which are consonants. Spell out one of the new words using only the foreign words for consonant and vowel. For example, in French a ruler (*une règle*) would be: consonant; vowel; consonant;

consonant; vowel. You could just focus on the noun itself and omit spelling out the article in a French or German word.

French: consonne/voyelle

German: der Konsonant/der Vokal

Secrets
Choose a secret flashcard and give clues in the language with: *I begin with the letter....* In a similar fashion, choose a secret flashcard and give clues in the language with: *I have two syllables.*

Over My Head
Ask for a volunteer to come out to the front of the class and close his/her eyes while you place a flashcard over the child's head. The rest of the class have to keep asking *What is it?* in the target language.

English	French	German
What is it?	Qu'est ce que c'est ?	Was ist das?

The child guesses which it is and the rest of the class announce *yes* (*oui/ja*) or *no* (*non/nein*) in the target language. Keep the choice of possible cards small at first to build up confidence.

Guess the Card
Choose a favourite card and the children have to put up their hands and suggest which one you have chosen. Each time they get it wrong, reply with: *No, it isn't...* so that they hear the phrase reinforced and how to express a negative.

English	French	German
No, it isn't that!	Non, ce n'est pas ça !	Nein, das ist es nicht!

Mixed Up

Stick a collection of picture cards on the board and a separate group of their matching text cards but mix them completely. Challenge children to match text and picture correctly, either as a whole class activity or a partner game.

Catch Up

This game gives good practice in combining reading and listening. On the board place a series of flashcards containing words in a list or making a short dialogue. You start to read on your own aloud from anywhere in the list working your way sequentially from there. Children have to work out where you are in the text and the game could continue in either of two ways. They could put their hands up to offer the next line from the list or dialogue and then you repeat the whole process. Alternatively, they all join in reading aloud quite softly as soon as they can until you change your place again and start somewhere else and the game continues.

Sticky Notes

Stick a series of flashcards on the board and place a sticky note in the corner of each one with a number on. You could play this in several ways. You can call out one of the numbers to the class and they call back the word on which the number is stuck. Alternatively, you call out one of the words and the children call out the number. Or you can play this as a team game: the children have to both correctly call out a number and say the word designated by the flashcard to get a point.

To extend this game, put the cards on a board *face down* and stick the sticky notes on the visible side of the card with a number on each one from one to ten. The children take turns (could be a team game) to call out one of the numbers and then, if the number is correctly said, they try to guess which hidden word is on the reverse. Give points for a correct guess and a few random bonus points for knowing the meaning of the word on the other side.

How Green You Are...

This is an old favourite. One person goes out of the room and the others choose a card and hide it in the classroom. The child comes back in and has to work out where it is, while the class sing a familiar song in the language, for example *Frère Jacques*. They sing softly at first and then more loudly as the person gets closer. When the card is eventually found, the whole class call out the word on the hidden card triumphantly!

Secret Conductor

This is another old favourite and is very effective for practising a series of whole phrases or question forms. Place on the board a series of shortish phrases you want the class to learn, for example on flashcards containing weather phrases, a brief dialogue or lists of food products, such as *a kilo of bananas*. One person volunteers to go out of the room or in the cupboard for a moment, while the rest of the class choose one person to be the Conductor. The volunteer comes back and all the class start to read aloud the first line of the text on the board, repeating each phrase over and over again until the Conductor gives a secret sign (i.e. a nod of the head, a wave, thumbs up) that they move on to the next phrase in line. The volunteer has to guess the identity of the secret Conductor. Everyone reads the text together at the end.

Wriggly Worms

Organise your class into three lines (worms) and ask them to face you. Give each child in the line a number. Each row will have a number one, a number two etc. Call out a number in the target language and the relevant children must reply. Show a flashcard quickly and ask what it is. The child who answers correctly first scores for their 'worm' and sits down. The worm which has everyone in it sitting down first is the winner.

Run to the Rhino!

This game works well when your class needs an active exercise which involves moving quickly around the classroom! Place your flashcards depicting themed nouns in various parts of the classroom (such on the board, in the corner, on your desk, on the walls). Divide the children into groups and give each group a number. Point to a group and ask the children to move quickly to the flashcard. For example, all members of group one run to the picture of the rhino and stand there, whilst group two runs to the picture showing the snake. To speed things up a little more, you could give the groups a number card and call out: *six – eight – ten: monkey!*

Find Your Partner
We often use matching halves of a flashcard when working with nouns and adjectives for example. One half usually depicts the noun and the other half has the word in the target language on it. Give half of your class a picture card and the other half the matching word card. Ask the children to walk around the classroom and find their matching partner. Once this has been done, mix the cards and play again.

Making a Move
A more active version of the game above can be played with flashcards and corresponding movements. Hold up a flashcard and ask your class to act out the word depicted. For example, with the topic 'weather' the children can be rain by running their fingers up and down like drops of water, or a strong wind by blowing hard.

Using Colours
The issue of noun genders appears in French and German very early on and cannot be ignored! Your class needs to understand which words are masculine, which are feminine and, in the case of German, which words are neuter. These genders are important for language accuracy and cannot be guessed. Neither are they the same in different languages. For example, the word *table* is feminine in French (*la table*) and masculine in German (*der Tisch*)! It is a good idea to teach the correct gender along with the new noun being presented and flashcards, especially ones you make yourself, can help with this process.

Many teachers use different colours to distinguish the gender of the noun. If you do this right from the start, you will help your children visualise the gender and learn associations in this way. It does not really matter which colour you use for which gender (red for feminine words, blue for masculine words and green for neuter words are popular choices), but the colours need to be consistent (preferably throughout the whole school too). You can write your colour-coded words below each flashcard picture and topic-related vocabulary can be colour–clustered, i.e. all the green neuter words can be presented together. Don't forget you can also display any new words on appropriately coloured card around your classroom to serve as a permanent reminder for as long as your display lasts.

CHAPTER 3
Quick Starts

Start your lesson in a lively, action-packed way to send the message that language learning is exciting and has lots of varied activities. Just as you have mental and oral starters for numeracy lessons, get the class in the mood for learning by revisiting vocabulary from the last lesson or plan a brief recap of useful language for the current one. There are many quick-fire little games to get the lesson started in this chapter and to help children to tune in to the language using minimal resources. Many of these ideas are generic and can easily be adapted to suit any topic.

STANDING UP GAMES

These are a great way to start your lesson. Wait until everyone is up ready and watching attentively before you start to speak or begin the game. This is always an effective way to establish good classroom control and to encourage children to be alert. They learn quickly to recognise your slightest signal that the game is about to start. You could tease children with a few false starts to a game by half raising your hand and then scratching your nose instead, or gazing obviously round the classroom until everyone is settled and concentrating.

Body Shout
Start with your hands at the top of your head. The children copy you. You call out a word or phrase and they repeat it. For the next word you put your hands on your shoulders and call, then your waist, hips, knees, toes etc. as they follow your actions and repeat. You could vary this by whispering or shouting alternately or building up to a crescendo when you touch the last body part. You can practise any vocabulary in this game: animal words,

greetings etc. or even the names of the body parts you are touching.

Star Numbers

This one is good for counting up to ten or further to thirty or in multiples of ten up to a hundred, whichever is appropriate for your class. All crouch down. Start to chant numbers together, gradually getting up, with a massive star jump at your highest number. Try to finish together in one big leap and shout.

Action Numbers

Another good numbers game. You face the class as before and chant numbers together in a steady rhythm but, on even numbers, everyone does an action which you've decided on in advance, for example, spin around, touch your toes. You can make this as complicated as you like as the class gets used to the idea. This is also a good game for children to do later in pairs or groups of three, making up their own actions.

Counting with Cards

You need to provide lots of opportunities to recite numbers forwards or backwards and also a chance to recognise them in random order or away from the context of just a string of numbers. Children stand in a circle. Give out number cards randomly around the circle (they could be up to ten or any higher number) and count aloud in numerical order briskly with children holding up their number when it is called, and then in reverse from the highest number downwards. Count again around the circle but this time following the random order of the circle, each child holding their card as a prompt. Do this lots of times with children doing different actions on each rotation, for example jumping in the air, crouching down, spinning around, all whispering and then shouting their own number etc.

Running Numbers

Following on from the previous game, ask children to change places if they have an odd number and then an even number or to run around the outside of the circle and back to their places. Next try calling for children with a multiple of five or two etc. or with the number two on their card. As an alternative to running, children could spin round on the spot or you could have the multiples of five spinning and the multiples of three running round! See if the class can identify which numbers fit into both these categories and what action those children should perform. (Make sure that you have looked in advance with children at the language used to identify these terms and work out what they mean. In French, the word *pair* for *even* is easy to understand.)

English
Change places if you have an odd number/even number.
Change places if you have a multiple of five/if you have the number two.

French
Changez de place si vous avez un numéro impair/un numéro pair.
Changez de place si vous avez un multiple de cinq/si vous avez le numéro deux.

German
Wechselt die Plätze, wenn ihr eine ungerade/gerade Zahl habt.
Wechselt die Plätze, wenn ihr ein Vielfaches von fünf/wenn ihr die Nummer zwei habt.

Up You Get
Call and repeat a sequence of words, for example the days of the week, months of the year, a series of numbers or just a list of words you have put up. Change how you stand for each word: start with standing tall and cupping your mouth to shout a word and then for the next word crouch down with your finger to your lips to make them whisper. You'll find all sorts of variations of actions for this game. Keep the pace lively and you can practise vocabulary and keep fit at the same time!

Alternate Numbers
Calling out alternate numbers or words in a sequence is effective too. You call the first number or word, the children call the next in

the list. Try the same words in reverse order. This is great played as a tennis game where you 'hit' the number or word to them and they send it back to you dramatically. You could make it table tennis, lawn tennis, football, hockey or whatever suits you. Again, when you've tried this a few times, children can play in pairs or threes.

Song Swap
Practise words on flashcards or colours by inviting volunteer children to come to the front to hold the cards. Everyone sings the word cards in order to a simple tune, for example *London's burning*. Then close your eyes dramatically while they rearrange their places and you sing the new song created by them swapping their positions. Start with a few cards and add a few more each week. If you don't want to sing, just chant the words together in different emotional tones or volumes.

Round the Circle
This simple group game is ideal for practising those introductory phrases which everyone needs, such as: *how are you; please and thank you; hello and goodbye; have a good journey or meal; see you soon* etc. Children stand in groups of five or so, with one person in the middle. The middle person goes round to everyone in the group, shaking hands and saying the chosen phrase with each partner. Each child takes a turn of being in the middle and initiating the conversations. You could choose the best group to demonstrate how well they speak or play it against the clock to see which group is fastest. If you choose the speed option, make sure that clarity is not lost in pursuit of speed; the point of the game is to learn how to speak clearly and communicate effectively!

Turn Around
Everyone stands in a space facing the teacher. This game works well for revising compass points or weather expressions, but it can be used for any other vocabulary which is distinctive, such as the days of the week, colours of the rainbow, numbers one to ten. Beforehand, put up flashcards of the chosen vocabulary around the room. Call out one of the phrases on the wall and ask the children to turn silently towards it. You could play this as an

elimination game or add a movement, such as *take two steps towards...*.

English
Take two steps towards...

French
Prenez deux pas vers...

German
Macht zwei Schritte in Richtung...

Map Work

Another way to turn the classroom space to your advantage is to imagine that it is the shape of the country you are studying. Set out for the children the compass points and perhaps put up signs for the four main directions. Then look at a map together and work out where the main cities/ports/seaside would be in the classroom. Children then stand up and you call out the compass points first and then the city names which they turn to. This is a more engaging way to learn the geography of the country and certainly catches adults out too!

English
North/South/East/West
Where is... the capital/the town/the port?

French
Le Nord/le Sud/l'Est/l'Ouest
Où est... la capitale/la ville/le port ?

German
Der Norden/Süden/Osten/Westen
Wo liegt... die Hauptstadt/die Stadt/der Hafen?

Mexican Wave

This is another very adaptable favourite which you can use with any vocabulary which you want your class to practise, and is particularly useful for learning a whole phrase or a question or short sentence. Keep it as fast-paced as you can so that children do not get bored.

Everyone stands up and recites the set phrase a couple of times together and then each person in turn says one word of the phrase in order on their own, right around the class. Each time, the person who says the last word of the phrase must sit straight down on the floor and is out. If you reinforce this with a hand signal rather than speaking, you will keep up the momentum of the game. Eventually you will be left with a couple of children in the last round and feverish anticipation and counting to see who will be the winner.

The standard football match version of this is to say the phrase around the room simply with everyone raising their arms in the air as they say their bit.

To the Left
This one contains helpful vocabulary to use every day, but is particularly useful if you are teaching prepositions describing place, for example describing where shops or buildings might be in a town, or classrooms in a school, or rooms in a house. Everyone stands in a space facing the teacher and spreads out both arms in front to face the direction called, for example *to the left, to the right, in front, behind, to the side, up, down*. Once children are proficient, they could do this in pairs.

English
to the left, to the right
in front, behind, to the side
up, down

French
à gauche, à droite
en avant, en arrière, à côté
en haut, en bas

German
links, rechts
vorn, hinten, seitwärts
auf, ab

Heads, Noses, Ears and Eyes

Sing together the familiar song of *Heads, shoulders, knees and toes*. There are many recorded, lively versions to sing along to on commercial CDs, but you can make up your own simplified version with just the body parts you need to learn, for example just the parts of the face or your head and four limbs.

English
eyes, nose, ears, mouth, chin, neck, hair
head, arm, leg

French
les yeux, le nez, les oreilles, la bouche, le menton, le cou, les cheveux
la tête, le bras, la jambe

German
die Augen, die Nase, die Ohren, der Kinn, der Hals, die Haare
der Kopf, der Arm, das Bein

Body Wiggles

Create your body wiggle to practise some body parts! For example hands (both held up, open and close fists), elbows (raise up and down), hips (wiggle to and fro), feet (swivel side to side). Children particularly like making up their own wiggles and performing in a group to the class.

English
hands, elbows, hips, feet

French
les mains, les coudes, les hanches, les pieds

German
die Hände, die Ellenbogen, die Hüften, die Füße

Action Verbs

This one is good for practising action verbs. Everyone stands in a space. Call out verbs in the imperative form (like a command) which have an interesting action to perform. Children repeat the word and do the action you demonstrate, for example, *swim, run, walk, jump, skate, sleep, dance*. (They particularly like seeing a teacher looking ridiculous dancing, so make that one a favourite.) Add new ones each week perhaps describing animal movements, such as *fly, slide, climb*. When they get the idea, add an adverb to qualify the speed of their movement, for example *slowly, quickly, carefully*.

English
run / walk / jump / dance / swim / skate / sleep
slowly / quickly / carefully

French
courez / marchez / sautez / dansez / nagez / patinez / dormez
lentement / vite / doucement

German
laufen / zu Fuß gehen / springen / schwimmen / Schlittschuh laufen / schlafen
langsam / schnell / sorgsam

Being Negative

When the class have mastered the previous game about action verbs, teach them the related game *I say do, you say don't*. You call out an action verb as before and then, after you all do the action for a count of five, they call back *Don't...* and stop moving, wagging their finger in the air to tell you to stop. This is a good game for teaching negative commands and children enjoy telling *you* to stop doing something for a change!

English
Run/Don't run!
Walk/Don't walk!

French
Courez/Ne courez pas !
Marchez/Ne marchez pas !

German
Laufen/Nicht laufen!
Zu Fuß gehen/Nicht zu Fuß gehen!

SITTING DOWN GAMES

Digit Flips
Every school has equipment for mathematics or science which could be borrowed to enhance language lessons. Have a look in your Resources Cupboard with a new eye to see what could be adapted. Digit Flips which hold cards of single digits to flip over to form random numbers are ideal for a quick recap of numbers. You can keep to single digit numbers or extend to two or three digit numbers, which children could then call out in the language. You could even target groups who think they are unbeatable!

What's the Time?
In a similar vein, if you're teaching your class about the time, get out the little clocks in your language lesson and practise (at least) the 'on the hours' in the language. As usual, you call out the hour and the children show the time on their clock. Then you show a time and they call out the time in the language.

English
What's the time?
It's ten o'clock/It's half past ten/It's quarter past ten/It's a quarter to ten.

French
Quelle heure est-il ?
Il est dix heures/Il est dix heures et demie/Il est dix heures
et quart/Il est dix heures moins le quart.

German
Wie spät ist es?
Es ist zehn Uhr/Es ist halb elf/Es ist Viertel nach zehn/Es
ist Viertel vor zehn.

Friendly Fans

In mathematics we use number fans, so why not use fans for
languages too? It's easy to make your own picture fans to reinforce
vocabulary you have taught (see Chapter 5, 'Being Creative').
Photocopied pictures, a laminator, scissors and a treasury tag to
hold a fan together are all you need to tailor-make them for each
subject and a couple of winter evenings to make them. Start with
asking children to show you a tiger etc., and extend to more elab-
orate questions when appropriate, such as *show me a fierce
animal, a brown animal, a tall animal* and so on. Children can play
the same games with a partner or a small group.

English
Show me a tiger/a fierce animal/a brown animal/a tall
animal.
What is this?

French
Montrez-moi un tigre/un animal féroce/un animal brun/un
grand animal.
Qu'est-ce que c'est ?

German
Zeigt mir einen Tiger/ein wildes Tier/ein braunes Tier/ein
grosses Tier.
Was ist das?

Drama Queens

Practise common phrases with a touch of drama to make the experience memorable. If possible, watch authentic clips of native speakers and discuss mannerisms, customs and the intonation of the spoken language to give you a foundation. One class loved learning *I don't know!* with a Gallic shrug and hands in the air. They would practise the phrase in a dialogue where they were asked as many questions as possible (which they did not understand) and they would reply to each one in the same way. Similar phrases could be *Look out! Go away! Help! I'm ill! Oh no! Oh dear!* Or you could teach your class to express delightful things such as *Enjoy your meal!*

English	French	German
I don't know	Je ne sais pas	Ich weiß nicht
Look out!	Attention !	Passt auf!
Go away!	Allez-vous-en !	Geht mal weg!
Help!	Au secours !	Hilfe!
I'm ill	Je suis malade	Ich bin krank
Oh no/Oh dear!	Oh la la !	Ach nein! Ach schade!
Enjoy your meal	Bon appétit	Guten Appetit
Good luck	Bonne chance	Viel Glück
Good journey	Bon voyage	Gute Reise

High Praise

In a similar vein, introduce praise words from the first lesson in a catchy way using thumbs up and expect the children to repeat each one cheerfully. Have a final both thumbs or circled victory sign for a favourite praise of the week. See also Appendix 3 for different ways to praise, encourage and be polite.

French
Bravo ! Génial ! Super ! Fantastique ! Très bien ! Excellent !
Bon effort !

German
Prima! Toll! Sehr gut! Wunderbar! Erste Klasse!
Ausgezeichnet!

Thumbs Up
Try to create an atmosphere of encouragement and willingness to
'have a go', using praise words and discreet prompting when
necessary. Invite a few volunteers to come out and recite any
newly learned phrase. After each recital, all the class put up their
thumbs and call out their own favourite praise word to congratu-
late them on their bravery.

High Five
Practise new words or phrases together by suggesting each child
repeats it five or ten times under their breath, counting off each
repetition on their fingers and then showing a High Five or Ten
when they have completed the required number. You can soon see
who practises thoroughly and no one likes to miss the possibility
of a High Five at the end!

Finger Dictation
Play a little dictation game where children sit in pairs or small
groups one behind the other. You call out a word or phrase you
want them to practise spelling and they use their finger to write it
on the back of their partner.

What's My Name?
Look on the internet together for authentic names of children from
the country you are studying and make a list on the board.
Construct a dialogue where everyone asks the question *What's
your name?* And then all reply *My name is...* when you point to a
particular name. Invite a volunteer to point to a chosen name for
the class to call. Children could then play this game in pairs. Add
teachers' names and have the children respond in an adult's voice

using the appropriate forms for Mr, Mrs etc. Practise formal and informal greetings such as casual words for *Hello Mr Green, See you later, Good night* etc. using all the names on the board.

English	French	German
See you later	À bientôt	Bis gleich
Goodnight	Bonne nuit	Gute Nacht
Good afternoon	Bon après-midi	Guten Tag
Good evening	Bonsoir	Guten Abend

Stick Them Up

Put up on the board a large picture of something you've been learning, such as a face. Position the words for the parts of a face randomly on the board around the picture. Invite volunteers to come out and place them in the right spot or play this as a team game with two matching pictures and sets of words. Face vocabulary is in 'Heads, noses, ears and eyes' presented earlier in the chapter.

Put Your Clothes On

This is great for practising colours and clothes. Put up on the board a large picture of a unisex body or two bodies dressed in nondescript underclothes. You could use the model in Chapter 5, 'Being Creative'. At the side, place a series of numbered cards with a picture of an item of coloured clothing on the reverse side of each one, hidden from view. Children have to choose a number, turn over the card and be able to name the item of clothing with its colour and stick it on the body. Having both a boy and girl body livens this up, as you can imagine the options available.

English

A blue dress; a green skirt; a yellow jumper; white trousers

French

Une robe bleue; une jupe verte; un pullover jaune; un pantalon blanc

German
Ein blaues Kleid; ein grüner Rock; ein gelber Pullover; eine
weisse Hose

Pass the Bag
You will need a bag big enough to hold a few flashcards (like a
wash bag you might take on holiday), preferably with a draw-
string so that the cards can be hidden from view and not fall out.
Everyone sits in a circle on the floor and practises singing or
saying a rhyme to the familiar tune of: *Hot potato, pass it round,
pass it round, pass it round. Hot potato, pass it round, pass the hot
potato*. Make up a simple rhyme in the language to fit the rhythm
as in the following examples.

French
Un, deux, trois, passez vite. Passez vite, passez vite. Un,
deux, trois, passez vite, passez vi-te (two syllables on the
last *vite*).

German
Eins, zwei, drei, reicht schnell herum. Reicht schnell herum.

As you sing or recite the rhyme, children pass around the bag which
now contains a selection of flashcards relating to the current topic.
When they reach the last word of the rhyme, the person holding the
bag must open it, take out a flashcard and recite the words on it or
say the words in the target language or do the appropriate action
etc. Place all cards back in the bag and continue with the song.

Guess My Name
This game works best if the class are used to the alphabet in the
new language, but if necessary you could just use our own familiar alphabet. As a prompt you could put up one of the posters
giving guidance about letter pronunciation and sing one of the
many alphabet songs from CDs. Alphabets in both French and
German are included in Appendix 1 of this book. Next, you choose
silently one of the words you've been practising for your topic
work, such as an animal noun or an action verb, which may be

written on a list in front of the class. You call out *I begin with the letter...* and they guess your word.

English
I begin with the letter...

French
Je commence avec la lettre...

German
Ich beginne mit dem Buchstaben...

Letters of the Alphabet

When you've reached the end of a topic and have learned a whole section of new vocabulary, this game is a good opportunity for a recap and can be played in pairs or teams. It might sound obvious but check first that your chosen letter fits some answers! Choose a letter and children have to think of an animal beginning with that initial letter or something to eat, a school subject, a colour or whatever topic you've been learning. The more possible answers there are the better, so choose common letters and encourage multiple answers. If you're at the writing stage, encourage the class to have a go at spelling the word, otherwise just collect words from spoken language. Your class may feel brave enough to spell the word completely in the new alphabet but, if not, keep to the one they know.

Who Am I?

This game works well if you have taught some vocabulary about describing people such as their hair, eyes, height or hobbies. Put up some scaffolded question forms to help children with the structure of their sentences. If necessary, work out the possible questions in advance with the class and practise them. Choose the names of five people to put on the board. These could be the names of teachers in the school or children in the class, for example. Next, select one secretly as your choice. Children have to ask clues to find out which is your chosen person from the five possible candidates, as in the examples below.

English
Is it a man/woman/girl/boy?
Does he/she have long/short/blonde/dark hair?
Does he/she like football/tennis?

French
C'est un homme/une femme/une fille/un garçon ?
Il a/elle a les cheveux longs/courts/blonds/noirs ?
Il aime/elle aime le foot/le tennis ?

German
Ist er/sie/es ein Mann/eine Frau/ein Mädchen/ein Junge?
Hat er/sie/es lange/kurze/blonde/dunkle Haare?
Hat er/sie/es Fußball/Tennis gern?

It Hurts!
This game reinforces body parts and practises useful vocabulary about being ill. Start with a picture of a face or a whole body, depending on what you have taught, and the name cards for suitable parts of the body/face. Invite children to match up the words and the picture and then practise a simple chant spoken all together such as: *Doctor, Doctor, I'm ill* or *Mum, Dad, I'm ill*. Next, you point to a body part and children chant *I've got a ...ache* in an appropriate voice.

English
Doctor, Doctor, I'm ill.
Mum, Dad, I'm ill.
I've got a backache, headache, earache.

French
Monsieur Docteur, Monsieur Docteur, je suis malade.
Maman, papa, je suis malade.
J'ai mal au dos, j'ai mal à la tête, j'ai mal à l'oreille.

German
Herr Doktor, Herr Doktor, ich bin krank.
Mutti, Vati, ich bin krank.
Ich habe Rückenschmerzen, Kopfschmerzen,
Ohrenschmerzen.

Where's My Bandage?

To follow on from the previous game, create some excitement by rigging up a place behind a classroom cupboard door or a curtain where a child can be handed a short bandage and asked to wrap it round a pretend ache on their body while the class guess where they are hurt. Alternatively, put plasters around parts of puppets or soft toys which are class favourites and ask the children to guess where the injury lies. This game is reflected in the Home Reading idea in Chapter 8, 'Showing the World', and presents effective ways to extend this theme.

How Much Is It Please?

Have a card on show with the question *How much is it please?* Next to it place a series of pictures of food or drink for sale in a café/shop/market stall with a price on each in euros. You can play this game simply as a price-naming game first. Everyone chants the question together and then you point to the food or drink picture and they reply with the price. When they have got the idea, make the question more difficult by adding the name of the food or drink in the question. Ambitious children could add a quantity such as a kilo of... /a bottle of... etc. or a flavour such as a strawberry ice cream.

English
How much is it please?
How much is an ice cream/a coke/a kilo of bananas/a
bottle of milk/a strawberry ice cream?
It's three euros/one euro fifty.

French
C'est combien s'il vous plaît ?
C'est combien une glace/un coca/un kilo de bananes/une
bouteille de lait/une glace à la fraise ?
C'est trois euros/un euro cinquante.

German
Was kostet das bitte?
Was kostet ein Eis/eine Cola/ein Kilo Bananen/eine Flasche
Milch/ein Erdbeereis?
Das macht drei Euros/einen Euro fünfzig.

Moving Café
After practising the vocabulary in the previous game, ask each child to choose one item for their own shop or café and a price for any item at all. They then circulate around the room and have a conversation with as many different people as possible. Everyone asks each new partner how much their own chosen item is, gets a reply using the adaptable price and then, in turn, gives replies to their partner. Before the children set off round the room it helps if you choose a confident person to demonstrate the dialogue with you so that everyone can see how it works. It is also a good idea to give an example of an easy choice of vocabulary for anxious children and of a more ambitious choice for adventurous people. In this way, everyone can participate comfortably and many children will push themselves to surprising levels when they see the possible answers. Encourage all the polite frameworks for a conversation, such as using greetings, please and thank you, Sir and Madam etc.

CHAPTER 4
On Your Feet

When you have taught and practised new vocabulary, you will want to explore as many ways as possible to embed the language in children's minds and it will help if you build up a supply of games which involve listening, responding and thinking about the target language. Some of the following games involve running around, some are team games and others require more reflection, but there should be something to fit every occasion, adding enjoyment and fun to the lesson. When you have tried them out, think back to the favourite games which you currently use as a warm-up in physical education lessons which require very little apparatus; it doesn't take much to tweak them into something simple and suitable for teaching a new language.

MOVING AROUND THE ROOM GAMES

Basic Moves
Whenever you have a game in a big space, set up a little routine which keeps children busy and active with few instructions. Start them off with finding a place and then get them moving with simple verbs, stopping at intervals to follow the next part of your game.

English	French	German
find a place	trouvez une place	findet einen Platz
run, walk, jump	courez, marchez, sautez	lauft, geht zu Fuß, springt
stop, dance, listen	arrêtez, dansez, écoutez	haltet, tanzt, hört zu
slowly, fast	lentement, vite	langsam, schnell

Number Groups Game

This game is a useful introductory activity for beginners, as you only need to know numbers up to ten or so and it needs no equipment. Children run around/walk/jump as usual according to your instructions, then stop when you call out a number and get into groups of that number. They have to join up and then wait for you to check by counting aloud with you.

Kebab Game

A more exciting version of the simple game above is to ask the children to get into groups of a given number, making a kebab on a stick. For this they have to lie down on the floor in their groups, but this time lying head to toe as close as possible in their kebab. The sight of thirty-two children trying to get organised squashing up alternately heads and then toes is enough to brighten anyone's day!

English	French	German
a kebab	une brochette	ein Spieß
get into groups of three	mettez-vous en groupes de trois	stellt euch in Gruppen von drei auf

Touch Blue

This familiar game uses vocabulary practised recently such as colours, clothes, parts of the body etc. For beginners, keep simply to colours. You announce *touch blue* and everyone has to move around the room and touch something blue on someone else (gently!). With older children, stretch to other nouns and gradually add more adjectives, for example, a left hand, blonde hair, a red jumper.

English
Touch…
…blue/red/green/orange/yellow
…left hand/right hand
…a red jumper
…blonde hair

French

Touchez...

...le bleu/le rouge/le vert/l'orange/le jaune

...la main gauche/la main droite

...un pull rouge

...les cheveux blonds

German

Berührt...

...das Blaue/Rote/Grüne/Orange/Gelbe

...die linke/rechte Hand

...einen roten Pulli

...die blonden Haare

Body Parts Game

Teach the words for three body parts (see also Chapter 3 for basic vocabulary). More experienced classes could have tricky ones such as ankle, elbow, hips. Children run/walk/jump around the room as usual according to your instructions and then you tell them to touch their ankle or elbow etc. The point is for them to place their ankle against the ankle of another person or a group of people together. When everyone is joined to another person, start off running, walking etc. again and choose another body part or even two body parts at the same time. This is an inclusive, co-operative game and works best if you encourage groups to let in as many people as possible.

English	French	German
ankle	la cheville	der Knöchel
elbow	le coude	der Ellenbogen
hips	les hanches	die Hüften
knees	les genoux	die Knie
shoulders	les épaules	die Schultern

Statues Game

Children move around the room following instructions such as *run/ walk/ jump* etc. until you tell them to stop and call out an instruction to do with early morning routines, for example: *brush your hair; get washed; eat a croissant; have a shower*. While they run around, you could play background music of a familiar song from a CD learned in an earlier lesson or a general CD of international music.

English	French	German
get up	levez-vous	steht auf
get washed	lavez-vous	wascht euch
clean your teeth	brossez-vous les dents	putzt euch die Zähne
eat a croissant	mangez un croissant	esst ein Croissant
have a shower	prenez une douche	duscht euch
brush your hair	brossez-vous les cheveux	bürstet euch die Haare

Wolf/Monster Game

One child is chosen to be the monster/wolf and stands at one end of the hall/room/playground. Others all wait at the other end and call: *Mister Monster, Mister Monster, how many heads have you?* S/he replies with a number, for example *three*, while his/her back is turned. The children take that number of steps towards the monster. This continues until the monster feels the children behind him/her might be close enough to catch. Instead of a number s/he calls out: *I'm hungry*, turns, and tries to catch a victim for supper!

English
Mister Monster, Mister Monster, how many heads have you?
Mister Wolf
I'm hungry

French
Monsieur Monstre, Monsieur Monstre, combien de têtes
avez-vous ?
Monsieur Loup
J'ai faim

German
Herr Monster, Herr Monster, wieviele Köpfe haben Sie?
Herr Wolf
Ich habe Hunger

Ladder Game
This is a hugely popular game and can be adapted to practise any
vocabulary, whether individual words or complete phrases. It's
particularly useful for words in a sequence (for example, days of
the week, months of the year), so that you can keep track of what
you've called. Otherwise, try to make a note of the vocabulary and
a tally because children soon feel aggrieved if they don't have as
many turns as their neighbour!

Children have to listen keenly for their word, prompt one another
and still have a chance to run about. This game works well with a
shopping theme where you start with practising language
previously taught by showing objects bought on your shopping
trip.

Children sit in pairs on the floor facing each other, with their feet
touching, making lines like the rungs of a ladder. Give each pair
the name of an object or day of the week to remember. You start to
tell a narrative about your shopping trip. Each time you say one of
the children's words, the pair has to get up, run up the 'ladder' of
children's legs, down the outside and back to their place. The
fastest back can score a point for their side of the ladder. You could
have two parallel ladders down the room to create a bit of competition and so that their words come up more often. You need to
establish a few safety rules however; keep your knees down, legs
together and make sure your arms aren't behind you to be trodden
on by the runners. If there is a child who cannot run for whatever

reason, ask them to call out some of the shopping words, adjudicate on the winners, keep the score etc.

The months of the year are presented in Chapter 1, 'Setting the Scene'. Here are some other useful words.

English
Monday, Tuesday, Wednesday, Thursday, Friday, Saturday, Sunday
a litre of milk
a kilo of apples

French
lundi, mardi, mercredi, jeudi, vendredi, samedi, dimanche
un litre de lait
un kilo de pommes

German
Montag, Dienstag, Mittwoch, Donnerstag, Freitag, Samstag, Sonntag
Ein Liter Milch
Ein Kilo Äpfel

Postman Game
Children stand in a circle with one chosen to be the postman. If you have a hat such as a little beret for him or her, this adds to the fun. S/he runs round the outside of the circle carrying a big envelope (if possible, get one ready in advance with a foreign-looking stamp, an Air Mail sticker and the school address written in the target language) while everyone else chants and slaps their legs: *The postman's coming. What time is it?* Then everyone chants the hours of the clock, for example, *one o'clock, two o'clock...* (see Chapter 3 for clock times). When midday is reached, the postman drops his letter behind the child nearest to him. That child chases the postman around the outside of the circle to try to catch him or her before s/he gets back to the spare place. The loser then becomes the next postman. The teacher can vary the speed at which they run by calling out *first class* or *second class* so the game can be played faster or in slow motion.

English	French	German
postman's coming	le facteur arrive	der Briefträger kommt
What time is it?	Quelle heure est-il ?	Wie spät ist es?
one o'clock, two o'clock	une heure, deux heures	es ist ein Uhr, zwei Uhr
midnight, midday	minuit, midi	Mitternacht, Mittag
first class	première classe	erste Klasse
second class	deuxième classe	zweite Klasse

Fish in the Sea Game
This game can be played with a parachute or just with everyone linking arms. Children stand in a circle holding hands loosely to make a fishing net or holding the parachute, raising and lowering the net with the waves. Three or four children are chosen to be fish and run in and out of the net. Before they start, the fish move into a huddle on one side of the room while the net circle silently decides on a secret number between one and ten. The net circle raises and lowers their linked arms (or parachute) to simulate a fishing net in the sea. The fish children run in and out of the circle as the net children count out loud together and, when they reach their secret number, they suddenly drop their arms/parachute to catch some fish children inside the circle. Any caught 'fish' have to swap places with some net children so the game can start again. You could vary this by using months of the year or days of the week or anything with a predictable sequence.

Fruit Salad
Children stand in a circle and the teacher tells them in turn one of four words to remember (e.g. four fruits/animals/drinks/colours etc.). When their word is called, those children run into the centre of the circle and change places with each other.

Reverse Game

All sit in a circle facing outwards. Give each child one of four words currently being learned and they get up and run around the outside of the circle when you call their word (as for Fruit Salad), but if you call *Midnight* or *Storm* (something appropriate in the foreign language to do with your topic) they have to turn round and back the opposite way. Only do this extra bit when they've shown they can be sensible in the first part! It's a good incentive for playing the game co-operatively.

English	French	German
midnight	minuit	Mitternacht
storm	l'orage	der Sturm
fruit salad	salade de fruits	der Obstsalat

Tap My Shoulder Game

This game is good for practising little phrases which add that extra something, or useful expressions which you suddenly find children have forgotten such as *See you soon; Thanks a lot; Have a good journey*. One class had forgotten how to say please and thank you: this game soon put that right! All stand in a circle and one child is chosen to go around the outside of the circle, tapping each person gently on the shoulder and saying the same one of two chosen phrases each time. When s/he reaches a person of his or her choice, s/he says the second phrase instead and then the two children run round the outside of the circle, back to their place. To add to the suspense, make a rule that each person is not allowed to choose their best or even usual friends; it is much more exciting if you cannot anticipate who will be chosen.

English	French	German
See you soon	À bientôt	Bis gleich
Thanks a lot	Merci mille fois	Vielen Dank
Have a good journey	Bon voyage	Gute Reise
Have a good meal	Bon appétit	Guten Appetit
Good luck	Bonne chance	Viel Glück
Good night	Bonne nuit	Gute Nacht
Hi!	Salut !	Hallo!

BEGINNERS' GAMES

Finger Puppets

You can buy packets of little animal finger puppets online very cheaply or even make some out of old rubber gloves (see Chapter 5, 'Being Creative'). You could also make some from card to use in class and give each one a suitable foreign name, as they are a good way of encouraging children to practise little conversations with each other. Even shy children can adopt a different persona with a puppet on their finger and feel confident approaching others in the group. Give out a puppet to each person and ask them to go round the room to say hello to the other puppets, exchanging their names, asking how everyone is feeling.

Soft Toys or Puppets

Most language teachers have special soft animal toys to use in the first few years with younger learners. You can use the animal to hold a regular dialogue with the class which you can build up over several weeks so that children start to recognise their part in the conversation. You can also throw the animal to an individual child and ask them a simple question to which they reply, for example, *Good morning/How are you?/What's your name?* Make sure you've practised this conversation first with the whole class and that you start with a confident child on their own to set an example before the animal makes its way backwards and forwards around the class.

Adjective Animals

A favourite way of using soft toys is to add a characteristic to each one to introduce extra vocabulary seamlessly. Sometimes you only have to look at a toy and you can see how a description fits it (for example, happy, sad, fierce). You could give the animal a title depending on the gender of the noun in the language (thus masculine nouns would be *Monsieur/ Herr* as in *Monsieur Singe/ Herr Affe/ Mr Monkey* and feminine nouns would be *Madame/ Frau* as in *Madame Vache/ Frau Kuh/ Mrs Cow*) and then always describe the animal with the relevant adjective when you introduce it each lesson. Another popular trick is to stick a plaster on a body part of each toy and explain that the animal has a backache etc. Children repeat what you say and learn: *Poor Teddy...*, *Take care*, and enjoy guessing which bit of his body is injured this week.

English
Poor Teddy / Be careful!
Mrs Cow is happy / sad.
Mr Monkey is shy / angry.
Mr Tiger is fierce / kind.
Mr Bird has backache / a headache / earache.

French
Pauvre Nounours / Attention !
Madame Vache est heureuse / triste.
Monsieur Singe est timide / fâché.
Monsieur Tigre est féroce / gentil.
Monsieur Oiseau a mal au dos / mal à la tête / mal à l'oreille.

German
Armer Teddy / Pass auf!
Frau Kuh ist glücklich / traurig.
Herr Affe ist schüchtern / wütend.
Herr Tiger ist wild / freundlich.
Herr Vogel hat Rückenschmerzen / Kopfschmerzen / Ohrenschmerzen.

How Many Times?

This is a good one to break the ice at the beginning of the lesson and can be adapted to whatever phrase you want the class to practise. Arrange the children in two long lines facing each other. Challenge them to see how many people in the opposite line they can say your phrase to in a set time (for example, thirty seconds) perhaps shaking hands each time. This is a good chance to practise those important questions which children need to know, but you could also use any vocabulary with this game, even *yes/no/please/thank you*. In this game you are not expecting a reply to the question, just practising the question itself. There are many introductory phrases in Chapter 1, 'Setting the Scene', and these three might also be useful.

English	French	German
What's the weather like?	Quel temps fait-il ?	Wie ist das Wetter?
Where are you going?	Où vas-tu ?	Wohin gehst du?
How much is...?	C'est combien ?	Was kostet...?

Traffic Lights Game

This is a variation of the traditional starter in physical education. Prepare coloured cards for traffic light signals in red, orange and green and call out the matching language instructions for the class to move to when you raise each card.

English	French	German
Get ready (orange)	Préparez-vous	Achtung!
Go (green)	Allez-y	Los!
Stop (red)	Arrêtez	Halt!

Shunting Game

This is a good one for practising directions such as *to the left/to the right*. All sit on chairs in a circle. A person in the middle calls out *to the left* and everyone keeps moving and sitting on the chairs in that direction until the opposite direction is called. When the person calls *all change*, they have to swap seats around the room. The person in the middle has to try to get a seat when everyone moves and then the person without a seat is the next caller.

English	French	German
to the left/right	à gauche/à droite	links/rechts
two places to the left	deux places à gauche	zwei Schritte links
all change	changez de place tout le monde !	Tauscht die Plätze!

You could add extra details, for example, *two chairs on the left*.

NUMBER GAMES

Shuffle Up Game

This is a good game for counting numbers, whether multiples of ten or straightforward counting or sequences of words, such as days of the week or months of the year. Children stand in lines of about ten or whatever is appropriate for your vocabulary. All face the front and, at a signal, start calling out their sequence in quick succession from front to back of the line. As soon as they get to the end of the sequence, the person at the front runs to the back of the line and they start again with a new person at the front. Carry on until everyone has had a turn at the front. The first group to finish and sit down are the winners.

Two versions of the old favourite Fizz Buzz

1 Stand in a circle and start counting around the circle in the target language. Any number which is a multiple of three or ends in three should be replaced by the word *Hello* in the target language and any number which is a multiple of five should likewise be replaced by *Goodbye*. Some groups may only be comfortable with numbers up to twenty, so adjust accordingly. Older children can obviously try more complex possibilities. This proves to be a good incentive for learning more numbers!

2 Instead of saying *Hello* or *Goodbye*, choose an action (for example, jump up in the air / crouch down) for the special numbers. Once you have tried some options, children could work in pairs to make their own sequences.

MORE SIMPLE COUNTING GAMES

Throwing Dice

Just use one die if you want to practise numbers up to six, or two dice to create two-digit numbers or to add numbers together. Throw big foam dice at random from one child to another around the room. All call out the number formed in the language. To make this more lively, each child could run all the way around the outside of the circle to get back to their place when they've thrown the dice.

Across the Line

Stand in two lines facing one another. Against the clock, throw the dice (or a ball or beanbag) across the lines from person to opposite person, counting out loud together. See if they can beat the target time which you set in advance.

Beanbags

In pairs or small groups, children throw a beanbag to each other and count how far they can go without dropping it. They could take a step further apart after each multiple of five.

Clapping Numbers

In pairs, children make up a clapping rhythm and count as far as they can, maybe spinning round after every multiple of five or crouching down and jumping up again after every multiple of ten.

Multiples

For more advanced groups, throw a soft ball around the circle and the next person must say the next multiple of two or five, or the next odd or even number.

Number/Dressing Up Game

When you have done some work on clothes or weather, this game is really handy. Gather together a variety of children's clothes in the biggest size available so that they are easy to put on in a hurry over normal clothes. Lost property boxes are a useful source, but don't forget to give them a good wash! Everyone stands in a circle with the clothes in the middle in a heap. Give each child in the circle a number up to ten in rotation. Everyone counts aloud up to ten in unison and then you call out a number and an article of clothing on the floor. The children of that number run into the middle, put on the appropriate clothes and do a lap of honour wearing the clothes before announcing to the group what they are wearing. They quickly take them off again before the next round. This game works well with just a series of hats such as berets, sunhats, sports caps.

English	French	German
clothes	les vêtements	die Kleidung
shirt	la chemise	das Hemd
trousers	le pantalon	die Hose
shorts	le short	die kurze Hose
skirt	la jupe	der Rock
dress	la robe	das Kleid
pullover	le pull/pullover	der Pullover

T-shirt	le t-shirt	das T-Shirt
coat	le manteau	der Mantel
hat	le chapeau	der Hut
tie	la cravate	der Schlips
I'm wearing...	Je porte...	Ich trage...

TEAM GAMES

Making Up a Team

Many of us still remember with a shudder being one of the last to be picked for team games as a child, so try to avoid that embarrassment whenever teams are needed. An easy and fun way to sort out a team to play a game is to prepare sets of animal name cards, or weather cards, or whatever subject is appropriate, and hand one card out to each child in turn, either as they come into the room or when you are about to play a game. Each person has to go around the room whispering their animal name or weather name etc. (with or without a mime to accompany it) until they find all the others in that group. They sit down as a group and from then on are *The Rabbit Group* or *The Sunshine Group* etc. A more riotous version of this is to ask the children to make their animal noise to seek out their group members and then ask each animal group to demonstrate their noise when they have got together!

Fly Swat

This game was inspired by a good friend who saw a collection of fly swatters in a village shop in deepest rural France and knew they would be ideal for an active language game. If you can't find two plastic fly swatters (sometimes you can find them in one of the trendy new kitchenware shops on the high street) then a couple of plastic rulers will do. Spread out one set of large-print word cards relating to the topic you've been studying on the board (or just pictures at an early stage of learning) and stand well back! Divide the class into two teams and ask one person from each team to stand a few paces back from the board with the fly swatter and run up and swat as fast as possible the word you call out. Encourage everyone to have a go and make sure you adapt your choice of word to the ability of the children. Have spare rulers at hand if you have a heavy-handed group!

Monster Match Game
Divide the class into two teams. Put identical monster body outline pictures on the board for each team with monster body parts (a range of different noses, heads, eyes etc.) stuck separately at random in the centre of the board. Choose one representative from each team, stand them in the starting position as far away from the board as possible. When the teacher calls out a body part (see vocabulary presented earlier in this chapter under the heading 'Moving around the room games'), the team reps race to find the correct part and stick it on their monster. As an extension, try adding a variety of coloured body parts, for example, call out *two red noses* for the team reps to find and stick on first. You could adapt this to any topic, for example, stick place names in the correct place on a map of the country or place animals in the correct zoo cage.

Monster Drawings
Children sit in a group or team with pencils/pens and paper. Prepare an envelope for each group with four or five strips of description for a monster written on them, for example, *he has got three black eyes*. Each group should have a unique set of descriptions. Children read and draw their monsters. When each group has finished, the children hold up their monster pictures and everyone has to guess what their instructions were.

English
Mr Monster has two big, red eyes.
He has three blue heads.
Mrs Monster has four small, yellow mouths.
She has five green noses.
He/she has six white ears.
He/she has seven black hands.

French
Monsieur Monstre a deux grands yeux rouges.
Il a trois têtes bleues.
Madame Monstre a quatre petites bouches jaunes.
Elle a cinq nez verts.
Il/Elle a six oreilles blanches.
Il/Elle a sept mains noires.

German
Herr Monster hat zwei große, rote Augen.
Er hat drei blaue Köpfe.
Frau Monster hat vier kleine, gelbe Münder.
Sie hat fünf grüne Nasen.
Er/Sie hat sechs weiße Ohren.
Er/Sie hat sieben schwarze Hände.

Medley Game

At the end of a section on sports, daily routines, school subjects or animals etc., ask children to work in a small team to make a medley of a couple of mimes. They could then perform these to their classmates who could guess which items they are showing.

Draw My Picture Game

Children sit in small teams with a mini-whiteboard and pen for each group. The teacher has a set of word flashcards of recently learned vocabulary which the children cannot see (these must be words that could be illustrated) and chooses one card secretly. One person from each team comes up and is shown the card, returns to the group and, without speaking a word, draws a picture to show the meaning of the word or phrase. The rest of the team have to guess the word, write it correctly on the board and then must read it in unison when all the teams are ready. Players take it in turns to get the next word to draw. Good topics for this are: weather words; body parts; breakfast food; transport.

Memory Game

This is a similar game with words instead of pictures. Teams sit together with a whiteboard and pen. One player from each group comes to the teacher, who displays very briefly a list of familiar items, made as easy or complicated as suits the class. The first player must remember as many items as possible from the list, run back and write them down as accurately as possible on the whiteboard without speaking. The second person then goes up to get the next group of phrases etc. Each player can only go up once. The winning group must have all the items written accurately in the correct order, and must be able to read them aloud in unison when they are declared winners.

THINKING GAMES

Word Claps

This is a great game to do when you are well into a topic, but it helps if you do a bit of preparation in advance to support children who might be anxious. You could play it as an elimination game or have a weekly session with a different theme to broaden the scope of the game. Everyone sits in a circle. You start by setting a clapping rhythm which children join in: two slaps on the thighs followed by two clicks of the fingers in the air. When the rhythm is steady, you start by saying a word from the chosen subject – for example *une glace/ ein Eis* for a food theme – when you click your fingers, and the whole circle carries on the rhythm seamlessly. The next person in the circle says a new word with the same theme, for example: *slap, slap, une glace/ ein Eis, slap, slap, un gâteau/ ein Kuchen*. Make sure you've talked about possible words or, even better, put up a poster of suitable vocabulary. Reassure the class that they can always repeat one that's gone before and have a few default options clearly on show, which are easy to say, such as *une glace/ ein Eis, une banane/ eine Banane*.

Another option is to go round the circle with the same food mentioned each time but a number in front increasing with each person, for example, *one sweet, two sweets, three sweets*. With older children who are accustomed to the format, ask them to add an adjective to their noun such as *a small bird, a blue bird*.

Menu Choice

Put up a selection of breakfast pictures and words which you have practised in previous lessons. Children choose their favourite three items, which should include a drink and a piece of fruit, and write them down. Individuals come up to the front of the class and the rest of the class guess their choices.

GRAMMAR GAMES

Some people may feel that this is a contradiction in terms, but it is possible to have fun with grammar! Try these sample games to practise the alphabet (French and German alphabets are at the back of the book in Appendix 1).

Alphabet Practice Game

All stand in a circle with a smallish soft ball. Start to sing/chant the alphabet aloud (there are lots of examples on commercial CDs to guide you with letter pronunciation) and throw the ball from person to person randomly, each throw making one letter of the chant. If possible, try to include every child just once in the routine. If you have more than twenty-six children in the class, keep going with a second chant until everyone has a throw. See how fast you can get through the alphabet and the class.

Scatter the Letters

All stand in a circle and randomly scatter a complete set of letters of the alphabet on the floor in the centre. Start by moving round the circle chanting or singing the alphabet and then invite the children to pick up a letter. If you have more than twenty-six children in the class, put in enough letters for everyone to have one and a few extra to give a choice.

- Chant or sing the alphabet again while each person holds up their letter at the appropriate time. Call the letters out of order and see if they can match the sound and letter this way. Rearrange the cards in the correct order and repeat the alphabet.
- Ask them to hold the card up if they are a vowel and then if they are a consonant. Practise saying the letters aloud.

- Hold up a familiar written word and ask them to raise their letter if it is in the word. Spell the word out together a letter at a time. Play a game, swapping places if their letter appears in a given word.
- Children join up in groups of about ten and see if they can make up words using themselves as the letters. Provide some blank cards (mini-whiteboards to write on) to fill in any unavailable letters. Make a list together of all the words discovered and see if there any letters which are needed more often such as vowels.

Word Games

In a similar way to the alphabet games, provide a selection of word cards in the target language. These may be nouns, adjectives, question words and verbs which you have practised. Ask children to pick up a word and then show you which word class it is by raising it in the air if it is a noun, verb, adjective etc. Play a swapping-places game for each word class, for example, change places if you are a noun.

Handy hint: it is possible to investigate making a sentence this way if your class have had enough experience with the language, but keep to what is within the grasp of the children. You could ask the adjectives to stand next to the nouns and discuss whether this makes a valid phrase. In French most adjectives follow the noun, except for very common ones such as *small* and *big,* whereas in German adjectives usually precede the noun as in English, but they must agree with the status of the noun and its gender. Continue asking children to make a longer sentence by putting pronouns first, then verbs, nouns, adjectives etc. Call out some of the words on the cards and the children raise their card in recognition. Continue around the circle so that everyone can see the range of words available. Children form small groups to make up phrases together and again use whiteboards to fill in any blanks.

As a finale for experienced groups, invite keen children to write as many combinations of words as they can find on a whiteboard.

As a reinforcement activity at the end of the game, ask children to place their card in a named word-class bag which you prepared earlier, for example, *a Noun bag, an Adjective bag.*

Slot Machine Game

Prepare three collections of picture cards on a familiar topic (for example cards containing the numbers one to ten, ten cards with fruit pictures, ten cards with colours) and ask three children to hold the sets in that order facing the class (i.e. one child holds the numbers, one the colours etc.). Throw two dice to generate a number and then turn over the first collection of cards that number of times. Continue generating numbers for each collection of cards so that you end up with a description, for example, *three/ strawberries/ red*, and say the finished phrase in the target language.

CHAPTER 5
Being Creative

Primary schools abound with crafty ideas and this chapter looks at 'doing and making' in the foreign language. Ideas range from making finger puppets from rubber gloves to creating your own aquarium, as well as designing word games and much more besides! All are straightforward to make and many can be combined with other parts of the curriculum such as art, literacy, numeracy, geography and science.

MAKE AN AQUARIUM

Figure 5.1 Make an Aquarium

This activity has strong links with a variety of topics such as: habitats; seashore; colours; animals; numbers; pets. It is both fun and simple to make and creates a marvellous display at the end of the day!

Resources: shoe boxes without lids (one for each child in the class); glue; paper fish and other sea creatures; paper fronds/weeds; cling film; differently sized stones/gravel/rocks from the garden; sequins, pieces of fabric and any other decorations available.

Steps:

1 Turn the shoebox onto its long side.
2 Decorate the walls and back of the box, either by painting them or by glueing some pieces of spare fabric to hang down to the floor.
3 A sandy base is appropriate and this can be made either with play sand mixed with glue or else by simply painting the base brown or yellow.
4 Now you need some fish and other sea creatures, weed and rocks to place inside the aquarium. The children can draw, decorate and position these items in their aquarium as they see fit and then glue them into place. You can glue the fish etc. onto the fronds and rocks as well, not just the back and sides, to give a more realistic 3D effect. You can create the same effect by suspending the fish etc. from the top of the aquarium on threads. Put some larger stones along the bottom of the aquarium too and glue them into place to weight down the tank.

English	French	German
fish	le poisson	der Fisch
starfish	l'étoile de mer	der Seestern
crab	le crabe	die Krabbe
shell	le coquillage	die Muschel
seaweed	les algues	der Seetang
octopus	la pieuvre	die Krake
lobster	le homard	der Hummer
seahorse	l'hippocampe	das Seepferdchen

5 When the aquaria are finished and dry, tape some cling film over the front of them. This gives a neat watery effect and also stops bits and pieces falling out!

Tip: the class aquaria make lovely displays and here is a song that you can all sing together as you show off your work (to the tune of *One Little, Two Little, Three Little Indians*).

French version
un petit, deux petits, trois petits poissons,
quatre petits, cinq petits, six petits poissons,
sept petits, huit petits, neuf petits poissons,
qui nagent dans la mer !

German version
ein kleiner, zwei kleine, drei kleine Fische,
vier kleine, fünf kleine, sechs kleine Fische,
sieben kleine, acht kleine, neun kleine Fische,
schwimmen in dem Meer!

MAKING A MOBILE

The sea-themed shapes from the previous activity also make an excellent mobile. Pictures should be decorated on both sides and then hung from a coat hanger around the classroom. The word in the target language for the hanging item can be stuck on the appropriate image, leaving an aerial record of the topic long after the displays have been taken home!

USING STICK DRAWINGS

A simple stick figure is easy to draw and it is surprising how it can add new dimensions and interest to your words. You don't have to be a brilliant artist and you can have a lot of fun with your class along the way. The trick is to keep things simple. You could, for example, encourage your class to learn to draw stick figures with you to illustrate the new language they meet. You can modify your stick figures as your confidence increases, but here are the steps you need to create a basic model. Your drawings will be most effective if you use a thick, black pen so that your pictures are really visible.

Resources: pen; pencil; paper; ruler.

Steps:

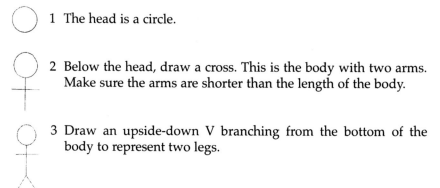

1 The head is a circle.

2 Below the head, draw a cross. This is the body with two arms. Make sure the arms are shorter than the length of the body.

3 Draw an upside-down V branching from the bottom of the body to represent two legs.

4 To create the face, draw a curve (a smiley face) or a straight line (a more serious face) in the lower half of the circle. Draw a dot for the nose. Draw two eyes by using dots or two circles with dots in the middle. Eyes that touch show fear or surprise. Hearts or money signs can portray other emotions. You can add some hair as well if you like.

Mega Manga (Sparrow, 2009) is full of useful tips for drawing manga-style, including emotions and hairstyles, which appeals to some children. Your stick figures can be useful too when it comes to talking about emotions in the target language and practising these when taking the register, for example (see also Chapter 1, 'Setting the Scene'). Here are some common feelings which you can practise by speaking in the appropriate voice yourself and/or asking the children to convey the emotions themselves using tone, facial expression, mime and gesture to help convey meaning.

English
I'm sad/happy/tired/angry

French
Je suis triste/heureux–heureuse/fatigué(e)/ fâché(e)

German
Ich bin traurig/glücklich/müde/ärgerlich

Your stick figures can become part of the classroom display too and used each morning to reinforce the language learned. Using this basic stick figure technique, you can branch out and experiment with other types of simple drawing. These two websites offer some lovely extension ideas (www.pinterest.com/ alwayslearning/doodles-and-simple-drawings and www.my-how-to-draw.com/how-to-draw-stick-figures.html), as does the website of the Campaign for Drawing (www.campaignfordrawing.org).

You can also try linking your stick figures to tell a story as in Figure 5.2, using speech bubbles to depict what the figures are saying.

Figure 5.2 Using Stick Drawings

Drawing your stick figures as part of a story or sequence can form the basis of animation, which many schools offer as after-school or lunchtime clubs. Such a project is described in detail in Chapter Two (Project 4) of *Living Languages: An Integrated Approach to Teaching Foreign Languages in Primary Schools* (Watts, Forder and Phillips, 2013).

RUBBER GLOVE PEOPLE

Finger puppets are very useful in language classes. They can tell stories and rhymes, they can have simple conversations and so on. An easy way to make one is from an old rubber kitchen glove – they come in several different colours, which adds to the fun!

Resources: kitchen gloves; scissors; glue; googly eyes; coloured wool; marker pen; decorations such as sequins, buttons etc.

Steps:

1 Cut the fingers from rubber gloves so that each child in your class has one.
2 Stick a pair of eyes onto each finger with the glue.
3 Add some wool hair. It is easier to do this if you put your finger inside to give something to press against.
4 Draw a mouth with the marker pen.
5 Add three sequins or buttons for clothes.
6 Use the marker pen to draw whatever details are missing.

Figure 5.3 Rubber Glove People

This website shows a short video of a rubber finger puppet in the making:

www.kidspot.com.au/omofunzone/Create-Finger-puppets+ 138+568+sponsor-activity.htm

Here is some simple language you can practise with your rubber glove finger puppets:

English	French	German
Hello!	Bonjour !/Salut !	Hallo!
Good morning	Bonjour !	Guten Morgen
Good afternoon	Bonjour !	Guten Tag
What's your name?	Comment tu t'appelles ?	Wie heißt du? Wie ist dein Name?
My name's... / I'm called...	Je m'appelle...	Ich heiße... Mein Name ist...
Where do you live?	Où habites-tu ?	Wo wohnst du?

LANGUAGE QUIZZES

Quizzes are popular with younger students and a short, regular language quiz provides a cultural context to language lessons. You could write five questions each week with an alternating focus on: geography (towns, rivers etc.); history (famous battles, events, inventions etc.); art (famous artists, paintings etc.); music (famous composers/musicians etc.); cultural/sporting events (include famous personalities); buildings/architecture (museums, landmarks); typical food etc. This is a fun way to impart cultural information which serves to ground the target language effectively. Here are two examples of simple quizzes you could use to promote class discussion in the mother tongue.

What do you know about France?

Discuss your answers first with your partner/group. Only one answer is correct each time.

1 What is the capital of France?
   a) Marseilles
   b) Paris
   c) Toulouse

2 What colour is the French flag?
   a) blue, white and red
   b) black, white and gold
   c) blue, red and gold

3 Which river flows through France?
   a) the Thames
   b) the Danube
   c) the Seine

4 Which of these food items do you associate with France?
   a) burger
   b) pasta
   c) croissant

5 In which other country in this list is French one of the main languages?
   a) Belgium
   b) Austria
   c) Sweden

Answers: 1b; 2a; 3c; 4c; 5a.

What do you know about Germany?

Discuss your answers first with your partner/group. Only one answer is correct each time.

1	What is the capital of Germany?	a) Munich b) Berlin c) Bonn
2	What colour is the German flag?	a) red, white and blue b) black, white and gold c) black, red and gold
3	Which river flows through Germany?	a) the Thames b) the Rhine c) the Seine
4	Which of these composers is German?	a) Bach b) Mozart c) Verdi
5	Where else in this list is German spoken?	a) Denmark b) Austria c) Norway

Answers: 1b; 2c; 3b; 4a; 5b.

YOU ARE WHAT YOU WEAR!

Making and designing your own clothes can be fun – and an effective way to learn the names of individual clothing items in the target language.

Resources: people cut-outs to dress; items of clothing to attach to the figures; pictures from magazines/the internet for the faces (optional); glitter, sequins, feathers, stickers etc. with which to decorate the clothing; adhesive putty; colouring crayons and marker pens.

Figure 5.4 You Are What You Wear!

Steps:

1 Children choose a figure to work with. They can draw in their own faces or that of their partner, or use cut-out faces from magazines/the internet.
2 Children select the items of clothing they will use from a central table. They should ask for them in the target language, for example *une chemise s'il vous plaît* or *der Mantel bitte*. A list of articles of clothing in French and German can be found in Chapter 4, 'On Your Feet'.
3 Children should colour in and decorate their figures and the clothes.
4 Cut the clothes out along the solid lines.
5 Fold back the tabs along the dotted lines and use adhesive putty to secure the clothes onto the figures more firmly if necessary.
6 Stand the dressed figures up. The children should now be encouraged to have simple conversations with each other following the examples below and keeping the language as straightforward as possible.

English	French	German
What is his/ her name?	Comment s'appelle-t-il/elle ?	Wie heißt er/sie?
What is he/ she wearing?	Qu'est ce qu'il/ elle porte ?	Was trägt er/sie?
He's wearing a shirt...	Il porte une chemise...	Er trägt ein Hemd...
What colours are the clothes?	De quelle couleur sont les vêtements?	Welche Farbe hat die Kleidung?
The dress is (yellow)	La robe est (jaune)	Das Kleid ist (gelb)
What are you wearing?	Qu'est ce que tu portes ?	Was trägst du?
My shirt is white...	Ma chemise est blanche...	Mein Hemd ist weiß...

BON APPÉTIT ! GUTEN APPETIT!

There are many opportunities in the primary curriculum to experiment with tasting or preparing delicious food from other countries and it's a chance to have some fun and learn about other cultures as well. This could be the culmination of a topic on food shopping, going to a restaurant, visiting French markets or a taster session before a school trip to France. On the other hand, many schools operate a continuous stream of work about healthy eating and this activity could fit neatly into a day or week of projects. The recipe presented here is straightforward and child-friendly. No cooking is involved and the healthy ingredients are easy to prepare.

Steps:

In advance:

1 Ask for a small contribution from the families of the class to buy the ingredients or ask students to bring in ingredients on the day.
2 Collect chopping boards, knives, aprons, spoons, bowls, a liquidiser, drinking straws and glasses.
3 Prepare risk assessments for chopping ingredients and discuss how to do this safely with the class.

On the day:

1 Prepare food-preparation space with a suitable table covering.
2 All wash hands before starting.
3 Read and decipher the French/German ingredients list together. Keep the English translation to one side until you have worked through the list.
4 Encourage students to read the French/German version of the recipe instructions and use the English only as a fallback.

Recipe for a simple milk shake

English version

Strawberry milk shake

Ingredients
Half a litre of milk
Three very ripe pieces of fruit from a choice of a banana or
peach or nectarine, six strawberries, small mango

Instructions
Rinse the fruit and cut into chunks.
Put all the chunks into a liquidiser.
Add the milk and mix well.
Pour the mixture into a big glass.
Decorate with strawberries cut in half.
Sip with a straw!

French version

Un milk-shake à la fraise

Les ingrédients
Un demi-litre de lait
Trois fruits bien mûrs au choix une banane, une pêche, une
nectarine, six fraises, une petite mangue

Comment faire ?
Rincez et coupez les fruits en tranches.
Mettez toutes les tranches dans un robot ménager.
Ajoutez le lait et mixez.
Versez le mélange dans un grand verre.
Décorez avec des fraises coupées.
Buvez avec une paille !

German version

Erdbeermilchshake

Zutaten
0.5 Liter Milch
3 sehr reife Obststücke – Banane, Pfirsich, Nektarine, 6
Erdbeeren, kleine Mango je nach Wahl

Wie macht man das?
Das Obst waschen und in Würfel schneiden.
Alle Obstwürfel in den Mixer werfen.
Die Milch hinzufügen und alles gut verrühren.
Die Mischung in ein großes Glas gießen.
Das Getränk mit halben Erdbeeren dekorieren.
Jetzt nippe mit einem Trinkhalm!

Follow-up ideas
1 Children could write out the recipe used and illustrate it. If they model their writing on a real recipe, they will begin to recognise the format of the genre.
2 Photograph the cooking event and make a display with the recipe and add captions.
3 Children can draw a picture of their own face or use a photograph and add a speech bubble with a comment in the target language about the food (see also Chapter 9, 'Starting to Write').
4 As a class, make up some more recipes in the target language with slightly different ingredients but the same basic foundation and create a cookery book together.

MAKE A WALL FRIEZE

Wall friezes are simple to make and serve as a permanent reminder of the new language introduced. Encouraging your class to notice the classroom around them is an important part of language learning.

Resources: a strip of stiff paper about 15 cm tall and as long as you need, with vocabulary labels in the target language.

Steps:

1 Decide on a topic for your frieze. The examples in Figure 5.5 are connected with 'transport'.
2 Decorate the bottom of your frieze. A black wavy line can be a road, or a golden line the beach, for example.
3 Paste your pictures onto your frieze, label them and then hang the whole frieze up where it can best be seen.

Figure 5.5 A Transport Wall Frieze

Transport vocabulary

English	French	German
car	une voiture	das Auto
lorry	un camion	der Lastkraftwagen (LKW)
police car	une voiture de police	der Polizeiwagen
tractor	un tracteur	der Traktor
breakdown truck	une dépanneuse	der Abschleppwagen
sports car	une voiture de sport	der Sportwagen
motorbike	une moto	das Motorrad

WORD GAMES

Word game formats are a motivating way to contextualise language learning, as they are often associated with fun, relaxation and pleasure. The examples below focus on the acquisition and practice of individual words and are easy to replicate in your classrooms. Why not incorporate some of them into your language lessons, using the models presented or designing your own?

WORD SPINNERS

A word spinner is a flexible way to consolidate topic-related vocabulary and helps children think about pronunciation in the target language.

Resources: a nine-sided disc; glue; cardboard; nine pictures; cocktail sticks.

Steps:

1 Make a nine-sided spinning disc using the template in Figure 5.6. Glue it to some cardboard.
2 Poke a hole through the middle with a cocktail stick.
3 Add nine pictures of topic-related vocabulary around the edges. The ones in Figure 5.6 are related to a rainforest topic.
4 Ask the children in small groups to spin the disc and say the name of the picture it lands on in the target language. They'll need to use the correct gender too of course!

Figure 5.6 A Rainforest Word Spinner

Tip: you could write nine letters on the spinner instead of pictures and ask your class to say a topic-related word aloud starting (or ending) with the letter the spinner lands on.

The rain forest / La forêt tropicale/ Der Regenwald		
English	French	German
monkey	le singe	der Affe
beetle	le scarabée	der Käfer
frog	la grenouille	der Frosch
butterfly	le papillon	der Schmetterling
parrot	le perroquet	der Papagei
snake	le serpent	die Schlange
spider	l'araignée	die Spinne
jaguar	le jaguar	der Jaguar
lizard	le lézard	die Eidechse

BINGO OR LOTTO

A game of Bingo always goes down well and the materials you prepare for this can be used in other contexts too. Playing Bingo is an effective way to help children remember topic-related vocabulary items and helps them to link spoken and written language. Typically Bingo is played with a sheet of numbers shown as figures which are called out at random and which are covered as they are heard. This version replaces the numbers with pictures which the children are asked to recognise in the same way, as they are called out.

Resources: ten counters (enough to match the number of pictures in the game); a Bingo sheet depicting ten small pictures with or without the words in the target language printed beneath them.

Steps:

1 Give each child (or group of children) a picture sheet.

2 Call out the name of one of the pictures, for example *die Kerze/ la bougie (candle)*.
3 Children should cover the picture with the counter when they hear it called out.
4 Repeat the process until you have said each word once. On the final word, children should have all the words covered and shout out *Lotto!*

Tips: include the gender of the word if you are using nouns as, in this way, word patterns are formed. Also, mark each word discreetly yourself as you say it to avoid a potential muddle at the end!

Afterwards children can be given the words to match to the pictures themselves. They could then rearrange the words in alphabetical order, which enables you to focus on simple dictionary work. Children can use their Bingo pictures to help them notice the similarities and differences between their own language and the target language, as well as focus on spelling conventions in the target language. You can look too at the way individual words are pronounced and encourage your class to imitate your model, either under their breath or aloud. Repeating the words rhythmically will help children link words and sound patterns together effectively (see also Chapter 6, 'Using Songs'). The example in Figure 5.7 is based around the theme of Christmas. Finally, you can ask the children to call the words back to you in a reverse procedure of the original game.

Figure 5.7 Christmas Bingo

Christmas words		
English	**French**	**German**
advent calendar	le calendrier de l'Avent	der Adventskalender
present	le cadeau	das Geschenk
Father Christmas	le Père Noël	der Weihnachtsmann
angel	l'ange	der Engel
candle	la bougie	die Kerze
snowman	le bonhomme de neige	der Schneemann
bell	la cloche	die Glocke
Christmas tree	l'arbre de Noël	der Weihnachtsbaum
reindeer	le renne	das Rentier
star	l'étoile	der Stern

WORD WHEELS

Word wheels take a bit of thought to construct but, once completed, are an effective and fun way of revisiting previously learned vocabulary. You could build on the words at the end by focusing for example on the way words sound compared to how they are written.

Resources: cardboard; pen.

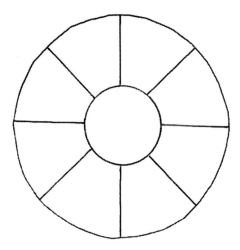

Figure 5.8 A Word Wheel

Steps:

1 Draw a circle on your cardboard, cut it out and divide it into eight segments.
2 In each segment write a letter and put one in the middle too. This gives you nine letters to play with.
3 Make enough copies for each child or small group of children to have a cut-out wheel.

Task: how many words can your class make out of the letters in the circle to do with topic x? You can use each letter as many times as you like and add any accents and capital letters at the end.

Tip: the shorter the words, the easier the task. The example in German below helps revise personal pronouns, whilst the example in French that follows the German one focuses on animals.

French wheel

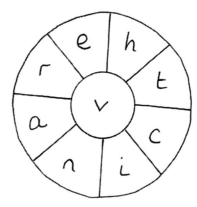

These animals are in the wheel (genders are not included this time): *la vache* (cow); *le rat* (rat); *le chat* (cat); *le chien* (dog); *la chèvre* (goat); *le ver* (worm); *la crevette* (prawn); *l'âne* (donkey); *la raie* (ray / skate).

German wheel

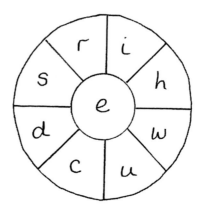

These personal pronouns can be found: *ich; du; er; sie; es; wir; ihr.*

WORD SEARCHES

A word search is usually a popular activity and one with which children are often familiar through puzzle books, newspapers etc. in their mother tongue.

Steps:

1 To make a simple word search which will help revise specific items of vocabulary, you first need to decide on a topic. If we take the topic 'fruit' as an example and work in German, then you need to find a long word for a piece of fruit. This will be the word which defines the outline of your word search. A good example in German would be *Wassermelone* (watermelon). You only need the noun in your word search and not the gender. Adding the gender could be a follow-on task for children once they have completed the word search.

2 *Wassermelone* has twelve letters. Thus your word search will be twelve by twelve squares wide and long. Place your word in a line vertically, horizontally or diagonally. Word searches are normally written in capitals and your class will be used to this format.

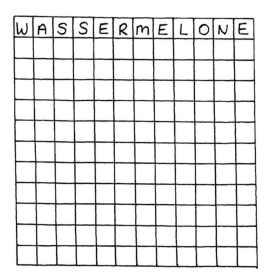

3 You need to decide from the outset whether you will write some of the vocabulary items backwards as well as forwards. There are no rules here but you need to take into account the abilities of your children.
4 You will also need to decide whether you are going to offer clues in writing, i.e. you provide the English translation of the words needed, or whether you are going to offer just pictures of the items needed. Pictures and writing are the easiest combination.
5 Once your first word is placed in the word square, add some other topic-related items which link to the original word on the grid.
6 Next add in some more topic-related vocabulary until you are happy that you have placed sufficient vocabulary in the word search. Our 'fruit' example now has eight items in it and looks like this:

W	A	S	S	E	R	M	E	L	O	N	E
	P								R		
	R								A		
Z	I	T	R	O	N	E			N		
	K								G		
	O			A					E		
	S		B		N						
L	E	F	P	A			A				
			N			N					
		T	R	A	U	B	E		A		
			N						S		
			E								

7 Complete the whole grid by filling in the empty spaces with random letters. Using letters with accents will make the task more difficult. Now add your clues and your word search is finished.

Eight pieces of fruit written in German are hidden in this word search. Can you find them? Draw a circle around each word when you do find it. Here are the words in English and a picture of each one to help you.

Words

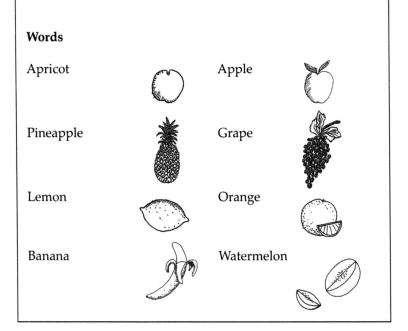

Apricot

Apple

Pineapple

Grape

Lemon

Orange

Banana

Watermelon

W	A	S	S	E	R	M	E	L	O	N	E
G	P	U	C	P	V	E	I	O	R	A	R
O	R	Z	L	Y	A	B	X	P	A	S	I
Z	I	T	R	O	N	E	L	T	N	R	K
V	K	A	R	H	T	N	A	Q	G	S	V
D	O	X	F	S	A	J	M	B	E	Z	B
P	S	C	W	B	U	N	Z	H	D	W	X
L	E	F	P	A	V	I	A	E	X	I	J
E	U	M	Q	N	P	D	B	N	J	U	E
B	I	T	R	A	U	B	E	O	A	R	Q
V	L	B	C	N	Q	K	N	E	P	S	U
A	Z	L	S	E	J	R	Y	C	U	T	H

Figure 5.9 A Word Search

CHINESE WHISPERS

This is a favourite word game and easiest to manage if the class is arranged in five teams of equal numbers (assuming a class of thirty children).

Steps:

1 Select one of your new words and write it on a slip of paper, one for each team.
2 Give the word to the child at the end of each team who then whispers it to the next child in line.
3 The children pass the word down the line as fast as possible until it reaches the front. The winning team is the one which is the fastest but which also pronounces the word most accurately.

WORD FANS

Word fans are a very flexible resource and can be used by individuals or small groups of children for a variety of purposes. They are easy to make and, if laminated, last a long time. Word fans enable children to demonstrate their understanding by responding physically to convey meaning. For example, the teacher names an item and the children respond by holding up the picture representing the word on their fan. Word fans also encourage simple communicative tasks, such as using the pictures to trigger questions and answers. In Figure 5.10, farm animals are displayed.

Figure 5.10 Pictures for a Word Fan

A simple question and answer routine could be:

Child 1: Was ist das? / Qu'est-ce que c'est ? (What is that?)
Child 2: Das ist der Hund. / C'est le chien. (It's the dog.)

Word fans can also be effective in a guessing game, for example where the teacher asks the children to guess the animal s/he is talking about by giving clues. The children hold up the correct picture in response to what they hear, as in the example below:

Teacher: *Je dis 'miaou !' / Ich sage 'miau!'* (I say 'meow!'); children display the cat.

This activity could lead on to some interesting discussion about the different sounds animals make in different languages.

Resources: a sheet of A4 paper; drawing pen/pictures; colours; treasury tags; hole punch.

Steps:

1 Fold a sheet of A4 paper eight times widthways.
2 Cut along the folds to give you eight long, separate pieces of paper.
3 Draw (or stick a picture of) a topic-related item of vocabulary on one end of each piece of paper.
4 Laminate each piece of paper to make it firmer and more durable
5 Make a hole with the hole punch at the opposite end to the drawing.
6 Link the eight pieces of laminated paper together with a treasury tag. You now have a word fan.

On the farm/ À la ferme/Auf dem Bauernhof		
English	**French**	**German**
dog	le chien	der Hund
cockerel	le coq	der Hahn
sheep	le mouton	das Schaf
horse	le cheval	das Pferd
cow	la vache	die Kuh
pig	le cochon	das Schwein
duck	le canard	die Ente
cat	le chat	die Katze
rabbit	le lapin	das Kaninchen

WHAT ARE YOU?

Figure 5.11 What Are You?

This game has stood the test of time in its various forms. The basic shape is sometimes called a 'fortune teller'. It makes an entertaining way of encouraging children to collect three facts to join together in one sentence. In this version, colours, animals and numbers one to eight are revised, but you could use any three topics as long as the end result makes some kind of sense (the sillier the better is sometimes most effective!).

Resources: one square of paper (typically 21 cm x 21 cm); a pen.

Steps:

1 Revise four colours, numbers one to eight and four animals in the target language. Leave these clearly visible throughout the activity. It is easier to choose animals with the same gender, as the adjectives will follow the same pattern each time.
2 Distribute the paper squares and ask each child to fold theirs corner to corner.

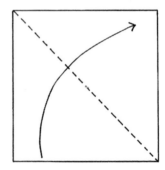

3 Fold the paper again to make a smaller triangle.

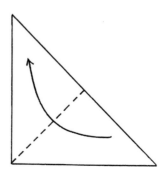

4 Unfold everything. You should have a square of paper with an X-crease across the middle.

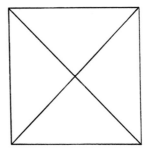

5 Fold one corner to the centre of the square where the X crosses.

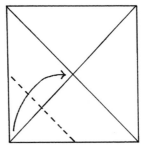

6 Repeat with the other three corners. You end up with a smaller square.

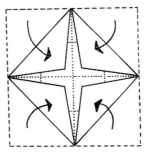

7 Turn the paper over and do the same action again with the four corners, i.e. fold them to the middle each time. You now have an even smaller square!

8 Fold and unfold the bottom edge of the square up to the top. Fold and unfold the left edge of the square over to the right.

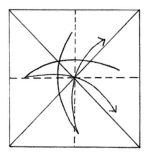

9 You now need to push the four corners of the square towards the centre and insert your fingers inside the flaps that form, creasing the folds back so that your fingers fit in nicely. It sounds complicated, but it is much easier in practice!

10 Your children at this point now need to open the whole square out again and fill in some language. Write four colours on the outside flaps in the target language. Write eight numbers from one to eight on the inside flaps and four nouns (animals in this case) underneath the inside flaps. You could colour some of the sections and/or add some stickers.

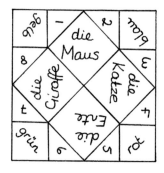

The children should now take a partner and ask him or her the following three questions:

English: What is your favourite colour?

French: Quelle est ta couleur préférée ?

German: Was ist deine Lieblingsfarbe?

According to the colour chosen, the flaps should be flapped once for each letter, thus spelling out the colour in the target language. For example, if yellow is chosen, the flaps should spell out G – E – L – B in German and J – A – U – N – E in French. Numbers are displayed next and the same principle applied.

English: What is your favourite number?

French: Quel est ton numéro préféré ?

German: Was ist deine Lieblingsnummer?

The child holding the fortune teller will flap the flaps until the number is spelled out correctly. Thus the number three, if chosen, will become D – R – E – I in German and T – R – O – I – S in French. Finally a favourite animal is selected and a whole sentence formed which can be written down and shared with the class.

English: You are a yellow mouse with three legs!

French: Tu es une souris jaune avec trois jambes !

German: Du bist eine graue Maus mit drei Beinen!

Of course, in order to spell out the word selected correctly, the children must know the alphabet in the target language (see Appendix 1). You could display it in your classroom during the activity.

CHAPTER 6
Using Songs

Songs and rhymes are bound to be one of the fundamental ways in which you teach and practise new language. They are often children's favourite activities as they can move about, sing in a group with their friends and make up actions to suit the words without really being aware that they are practising new vocabulary. You can make the experience new and refreshing each time you introduce a song by varying the actions they add, how loudly or softly they sing each line or verse, whether they are standing up or sitting down, whether they sing in groups or not etc. Although some adults are naturally reluctant to sing out on their own, children have few qualms about joining in and enjoy the challenge of singing in rounds or parts. Starting a lesson with a song, especially one with lively actions or which involves moving around the room to greet other people, is a great bonus. It sends an immediate message that this is a different kind of lesson full of vitality and enjoyment and emphasises the fun of communicating with others. It is truly astonishing how many children remember key vocabulary through the songs they have learned in their language lessons!

In time you may find that a small language choir emerges from a combination of classes or from the enthusiasm of individual children; recording a CD of language songs produced by your choir or class often proves to be a popular way of spreading the word about languages and a money spinner for school funds. Over the last few years, choirs have become more popular both in and out of schools and there has been a lot of publicity about the physical, intellectual and social benefits of singing. Many schools have thriving choirs these days, so why not combine the two and set up a language-based group of your own?

Over time you will need to set up a collection of resources, which should include a variety of song compilations. It is important to build up a mixture of authentic songs sung by native speakers of the language, as well as having a few commercially made language CDs which are suitable for the age group you teach. Probably the largest supply of songs will be those you make up yourself; they will cost nothing at all and be purpose-made to fit the kind of children you teach and the subjects you are working on.

AUTHENTIC SONGS

Listening to authentic songs is a crucial early-learning experience which is easy to neglect. If you think back to how we all learned our mother tongue, we were exposed to years of absorbing the shape and sound of our language before we were able to express ourselves, and children should be given time to take in this flow and colour almost as background music. In this way, they will hold in their memory the intonation needed for the shape of a sentence, for the formation of a question, for the general rumble of a conversation in the new language. When you go to a new country it is fascinating to sit back and listen to the shapes of conversations going on around you and notice the difference between the sounds of different languages. This is the background hum which young learners need to tune into. Make use of every chance to play a song for a couple of minutes during each language lesson or incorporate one into the normal school day by having a suitable track playing whenever children are waiting for the register to be called, getting changed for physical education or lining up at the door.

These songs are often nursery rhymes or traditional songs just like the ones we all learned in childhood. They often have catchy, easy tunes, short lyrics, often with a chorus, and a bouncy style just right for bouncing a toddler on your knee. Young language learners could move about to them or perform actions and listen for particular sounds or join in the words displayed on a whiteboard. Look online (see for example www.little-linguist.co.uk) for suitable collections.

PURPOSE-MADE COMMERCIAL CDS

There are many commercial CDs on the market targeted at teaching primary school children, which cover all the main subject areas you will need and have lively and catchy tunes which are easy to pick up. Some have a sung track followed by a karaoke melody, which enables you to practise to a backing track immediately, and all have the words available for you to practise and reproduce. Some come as part of a complete package of a language scheme for different years of learning and provide follow-up suggestions.

HOME-MADE SONGS

These songs have the benefit of being free, purpose-built and tailor-made to suit your own class and your current topic. The first step is to find a straightforward tune which you know well enough to sing on your own which is also familiar to the children. Think back to traditional childhood songs which everybody knows and which could be adapted easily. The following tunes are some of our favourites for making up songs. Most children know them, the lines are fairly short and they have a catchy rhythm. The first two are obvious but that is no accident; they are easy to adapt to simple vocabulary and quick to learn.

Frère Jacques
London's Burning
You Are My Sunshine
She'll Be Coming Round the Mountain
Jingle Bells
Here We Go Round the Mulberry Bush
Polly Put the Kettle On
If You're Happy and You Know It...
London Bridge Is Falling Down
Bobby Shaftoe
Agadoo
Oh, Oh, Oh, How Good Is the Lord
Nice One, Cyril
We Wish You a Merry Christmas

On the First Day of Christmas
How Much Is That Doggy in the Window?
There's a Hole in my Bucket
Lavender's Blue
The Farmer's in His Den
Heads, Shoulders, Knees and Toes
The Animals Went in Two by Two
Red and Yellow and Pink and Green
Hot Cross Buns
Oh the Grand Old Duke of York
Three Blind Mice
Oh Dear, What Can the Matter Be?
Baa Baa Black Sheep
I Had a Little Nut Tree
Sur le pont d'Avignon.

Teaching with songs

1 Use a familiar tune and add some simple words. Use as much repetition as possible so that it is accessible to everyone. If it helps, you could put the text up for the children to see as they sing.
2 Hum the tune first and use your hands to encourage everyone to hum with you so that they have got past the embarrassment of singing! Then *you* sing it on your own all the way through with the words.
3 Teach it line by line and keep practising it in manageable chunks.
4 When the children have mastered the basic song, look for possible actions or mimes to make it as lively and fun as you can.

One option to turn an ordinary song into something special is to turn it into a round by dividing the group into two or three sections to begin in sequence. It is easy to train a class to sing in a round and to make it clear that they will always sing it all the way through twice. Singing a song in the target language as a round is certainly impressive for an assembly or a small performance in front of a parallel class or a visitor!

Impromptu songs

It is also easy to make up a song on the spot as part of your lesson. Put up flashcards of your topic in front of the class or on the whiteboard in any order. Practise saying the words in the usual ways (see Chapter 2, 'Using Flashcards' for examples) and then hum the tune you want to use, inviting the children to hum with you. Next, point in turn to each card, singing the words to the tune. Start by just going between two or three cards at first, trying to catch the children out when you unexpectedly repeat one card several times on the run. When they are familiar with this, extend the song by pointing to different cards in succession to fit each part of the tune. This works well because children have to be alert to see what is coming next and they enjoy it if you play little games to go from one end of the cards to the other or if you choose funny repetitions. As a follow-up you could invite a child to come up and choose cards for the song or give the children a topic fan and ask them to sing in pairs when they pick each card.

Bringing your songs to life

A kinaesthetic approach to performing these songs helps to reinforce the language and makes the subject more inclusive. Adding a sociable element also helps to integrate children more fully with their classmates and makes sure that no one is left out.

The easiest songs for you to make up yourself matching words to movements are greetings, such as *Hello, Good morning/ evening/ afternoon, Goodbye, How are you? What's your name?* With these essential phrases you can combine a simple greeting with a friendly movement. If you want to limit any moving about, ask children to turn to their neighbour first on one side and then the other and shake hands as they sing, then turn around to the people in front and behind.

Singing round a circle

If you have more space, another way is to ask half the class to make a circle and then ask the rest of the class to stand behind someone in the circle. The inner people then turn round to face the outer people and you have a set of two concentric rings and ready-made partners. Each set of partners sings the song, shaking hands, and then the outer circle rotates to the left, one person at a time, to sing with a new partner the next time etc. In this way you can practise a useful phrase many times, you discover a new unexpected partner each time and, significantly, no one is left out.

Quick-change songs
A third method is to ask everyone to find a space to stand in with a partner or two, making sure that no one is left out. Sing the song once and then on the count of *one, two, three*, each person has to run to a different partner or partners. Keep a rule that groups should look out for stray people to join up with or that the teacher stands in an obvious place as a partner for anyone caught out on their own.

Added extras
Children could also perform in pairs or small groups and add any action as they sing, such as clapping the next word, touching their head, spinning round, jumping in the air, doing a high five, in any combination which suits the age of the class. Add a few choruses for your lyrics, by practising *Oh No! Yes, yes! Yes, it's true! No, it's false!* Or look out for praise words which can be inserted to add vigour such as: *Hooray; Great; Fantastic!*

English
Oh No! / Yes, it's true / No, it's false / Hooray / Great / Fantastic!

French
Mais non ! / Oui c'est vrai / Non c'est faux / Bravo / Génial / Fantastique !

German
Aber nein! / Ja, das ist wahr / Nein, das ist falsch / Hurra / toll / prima!

Questions and answers
Another series of songs could be devoted to questions and answers, where children line up opposite each other and one side

calls out the question as a chorus and the other side replies. This could then lead to paired work as above where children rotate around the class and ask each other the question and answer their partner's question in turn. It is important to give time to practising question forms as they are often overlooked, as it is the teacher who often is the one who asks the question in the normal classroom routine, whilst the children provide the answer. Useful questions would be: *What's your name? How are you? How old are you? Where do you live? What time is it? Where are you going? What are you doing? How much is it? What is that?*

French
Comment tu t'appelles ? Comment ça va ? Quel âge as-tu ? Où habites-tu ? Quelle heure est-il ? Où vas-tu ? Que fais-tu ? C'est combien ? Qu'est-ce que c'est ?

German
Wie heißt du? Wie geht's? Wie alt bist du? Wo wohnst du? Wie spät ist es? Wohin gehst du? Was machst du? Was kostet das? Was ist das?

THEMED SONGS

We have chosen some popular themes for examples of easy song structures. Try them out with your class, adapt them to the topics you are teaching and then you will imagine songs everywhere! Put the words on your whiteboard and sing them when you're lining up or getting dressed for physical education. The translations of the songs that follow are not word-for-word, as the important thing is that the songs scan properly. But the topics are the same in each case and we have tried to fit the words as closely as possible. There is always room for poetic licence, remember!

Food is a good starting point for a simple song and always appeals to children.

Breakfast songs
Start with the simplest ideas and lots of repetition, for example a few common words for breakfast food. Point to the picture cards, do eating and drinking actions or hold up real food to prompt. With all these songs, you could start by repeating only one line all the way through and then build up to extra lines when you feel that the children are ready.

Tune of *Jingle Bells*

French
Un croissant, un croissant
Un pain au chocolat
Des céréales, de la confiture   (cereal, jam)
Un chocolat chaud pour moi.   (hot chocolate for me)

German
Ein Glas Milch, ein Glas Milch   (glass of milk)
Eine Tasse Tee   (cup of tea)
Zwei Brötchen mit Käse darauf   (two rolls with cheese)
Orangensaft für mich.   (orange juice)

Tune of *London's Burning*

French
J'ai un croissant, j'ai un croissant
J'ai du pain, j'ai du pain   (I've got some bread)
Encore du beurre, encore   (more butter)
du beurre
Moi, j'ai faim, moi, j'ai faim !   (I'm hungry)

German
Ich habe Brötchen, ich habe   (I've got some rolls)
Brötchen
Ich esse ein Ei, ich esse ein Ei   (I'm eating an egg)
Mit Marmelade, mit   (with jam)
Marmelade
Ich habe Hunger, ich habe   (I'm hungry)
Hunger.

Tune of *Frère Jacques*

French

Je bois du café x 2	(I drink coffee)
Je mange un croissant chaud x 2	(I eat a warm croissant)
Je prends le petit déjeuner x 2	(I have breakfast)
Bon appétit !	

German

Ich trinke Kaffee, ich trinke Kaffee	(I drink coffee)
Ich esse ein Ei, ich esse ein Ei	(I eat an egg)
Wir frühstücken zusammen,	(We eat breakfast
wir frühstücken zusammen	together)
Guten Appetit!	

You could extend the idea by adding some days of the week and inviting children to choose some food each day.

Tune of *There's a Hole in My Bucket*

French

Pour mon petit déjeuner,	(For my breakfast)
Le lundi, le lundi	(on Monday)
Pour mon petit déjeuner	
Je prends un croissant.	(I have a croissant)
Pour mon petit déjeuner	
Le mardi, le mardi	(on Tuesday)
Pour mon petit déjeuner,	
Je prends une banane.	(I have a banana)

German

Für mein Frühstück am Montag,	(For my breakfast)
am Montag, am Montag	(on Monday)
Für mein Frühstück am Montag	
Esse ich gern Müsli.	(I like eating muesli)
Für mein Frühstück am Dienstag,	
am Dienstag, am Dienstag	(on Tuesday)
Für mein Frühstück am Dienstag	
Esse ich gern Joghurt.	(I like eating yoghurt)

...and so on, through the rest of the weekdays.

More complicated breakfast songs

Or for more advanced groups, try adding a time to the mix and more detail about the food or drink.

Tune of *Here We Go Round the Mulberry Bush*

French

Lundi, je bois un chocolat chaud,	(On Monday I drink a hot chocolate)
un chocolat chaud, un chocolat chaud.	
Lundi je bois un chocolat chaud	
À sept heures et demie.	(at half past seven)
Mardi, je bois un jus d'orange,	(On Tuesday I drink orange juice)
un jus d'orange, un jus d'orange	
Mardi je bois un jus d'orange	
À sept heures et demie.	

German

Montag trinke ich eine heiße Schokolade,	(On Monday I drink a hot chocolate)
eine heiße Schokolade, eine heiße Schokolade,	
Montag trinke ich eine heiße Schokolade,	
Um halb acht am Morgen	(at half past seven in the morning)
Dienstag trinke ich Orangensaft,	(On Tuesday I drink orange juice)
Orangensaft, Orangensaft,	
Dienstag trinke ich Orangensaft,	
Um halb acht am Morgen	(at half past seven in the morning)

...and continue through the week, changing the drink/food and time too if it is appropriate.

Another lively option is to add a chorus. Think up some actions and a rousing finale.

Tune of *She'll Be Coming Round the Mountain*

French

Je voudrais un croissant, oui	(I would like a croissant,
c'est vrai (thumbs up)	yes it's true)
Je voudrais du beurre...	(I would like some butter)
Je voudrais du pain...	(I would like some bread)
Je voudrais manger tout de	(I would like
suite, oui c'est vrai !	to eat straightaway)

German

Ich hätte gern ein Brötchen,	(I'd like a bread roll,
aber wirklich! (thumbs up)	yes really!)
Ich hätte gern die Butter...	(I would like some butter)
Ich hätte gern das Brot...	(I would like some bread)
Ich habe großen Hunger, aber	(I'm really hungry, yes,
wirklich!	truly!)

With this one, you could just sing the same line all the way through to make separate verses and add *oui, c'est vrai* at the end of each line or *aber wirklich!* rising to a crescendo on the last *oui, c'est vrai !* or *aber wirklich!* You could also vary it by encouraging children to say what they don't like, or at the end of the line they could substitute *non, c'est faux !* or *nein, nicht wahr!* (no, it's not true).

The next format gives you the chance to add the name of a teacher or child in the school and an appropriate (or inappropriate) food or drink along with a useful final phrase. You could vary this with other expressions such as *Goodbye, Good luck, See you soon.*

Tune of *Sur le pont d'Avignon*

French

Monsieur Jacques mange les frites	(Mr Jacques eats chips)
Tous les lundis, tous les lundis	(every Monday)
Monsieur Jacques mange les frites	
Tous les lundis. Bon appétit !	
Monsieur Jacques mange les glaces	(eats ice cream every Tuesday)
Tous les mardis, tous les mardis etc.	

German

Herr Steinwald isst gern Pommes,	(Mr Steinwald likes eating chips)
Jeden Montag, jeden Montag,	(every Monday)
Herr Steinwald isst gern Pommes,	
Jeden Montag. Guten Appetit!	
Fräulein Schwarz isst gern Eis,	(Miss Black likes eating ice cream)
Jeden Montag, jeden Montag etc.	

Tune of *If You're Happy and You Know It*
Everyone knows this song; it works well in a circle and is a good choice for adding actions.

French

Si tu aimes les bananes, tape tes mains x 2	(If you like bananas, clap your hands)
Si tu aimes les bananes, tu aimes les bananes,	
Tu aimes les bananes, tape tes mains.	
Si tu aimes les cerises, touche ta tête x 2	(If you like cherries, touch your head)
Si tu aimes les fraises, claque tes doigts x 2	(If you like strawberries, click your fingers)

German

Wenn du Bananen gern isst,	(If you like bananas,
Hände hoch! x 2	put your hands up)
Wenn du Bananen gern isst,	
Bananen gern ißt,	
Wenn du Bananen gern isst,	
Hände hoch!	
Wenn du Kirschen gern isst,	(If you like cherries,
berührt den Kopf! x 2	touch your head)
Wenn du Erdbeeren gern isst,	(If you like strawberries,
schnippt mit den Fingern! x 2	click your fingers)

Hobbies and routines songs

Hobbies or daily routines work well in song form; here are two simple ones to start with. Remember that if this is too much vocabulary in one go, just keep to one line all the way through.

Tune of *Three Blind Mice*

French

Je joue au foot x 2	(I play football)
Je fais du vélo x 2	(I go cycling)
Je fais de la natation x 2	(I go swimming)
Je suis fatigué(e) x 2	(I'm tired)

German

Ich spiele Fußball x 2	(I play football)
Ich fahre Rad x 2	(I go cycling)
Ich schwimme sehr oft x 2	(I go swimming a lot)
Ich bin müde	(I'm tired)

Tune of *London's Burning*

French

Je me lève x 2	(I get up)
Je me lave x 2	(I get washed)
Je me brosse les dents x 2	(I brush my teeth)
Je m'habille x 2	(I get dressed)

German

Ich stehe auf x 2	(I get up)
Ich wasche mich x 2	(I get washed)
Ich putze die Zähne x 2	(I brush my teeth)
Ich ziehe mich an x 2	(I get dressed)

Tune of *Here We Go Round the Mulberry Bush*
This is a useful tune as it gives you scope for longer sentences. It could be sung as a question-and-answer song with half the class singing each part and suitable actions for the hobbies.

French

Qu'est-ce que tu fais ce soir ? x 2	(What are you doing this evening?)
Qu'est-ce que tu fais ce soir ?	
Je fais de la lecture.	(I'm reading)

Subsequent verses could end in:

Je fais du foot	(playing football)
Je fais du vélo	(cycling)
Je joue aux cartes	(playing cards)
Je fais du ski	(skiing)
Je joue du piano etc.	(playing the piano)

German

Was machst du heute Abend? x 2	(What are you doing this evening?)
Was machst du heute Abend?	
Ich lese ein Buch	(I'm reading a book)

Subsequent verses could end in:

Ich spiele Fußball	(playing football)
Ich fahre Rad	(cycling)
Ich spiele Karten,	(playing cards)
Ich fahre Ski	(skiing)
Ich spiele Klavier etc.	(playing the piano)

Weather and seasons songs
Tune of *Frère Jacques*

French

Il fait froid x 2	(It's cold)
Il fait chaud x 2	(It's hot)
Il neige, il pleut	(It's snowing, it's raining)
Quel temps fait-il aujourd'hui ?	(What's the weather like today?)

German

Es ist kalt x 2	(It's cold)
Es ist heiß x 2	(It's hot)
Es regnet, es schneit	(It's snowing, it's raining)
Wie ist das Wetter heute?	(What's the weather like today?)

Tune of *Frère Jacques* again
A little seasons song:

French

Printemps, été x 2	(Spring, summer)
Automne, hiver x 2	(autumn, winter)
Sont les quatre saisons x 2	(are the four seasons)
Printemps, été	
Automne, hiver.	

German

Frühling, Sommer x 2	(spring, summer)
Herbst und Winter x 2	(autumn and winter)
Sind die vier Jahreszeiten x 2	(are the four seasons)
Frühling, Sommer	
Herbst und Winter.	

Tune of *I Will Make You Fishers of Men*
A more complicated song is based around this tune:

French

Je vais faire un bonhomme de neige	(I'm going to make a snowman)
Un bonhomme de neige, un bonhomme de neige	
Je vais faire un bonhomme de neige	
En hiver.	(in winter)
Je vais mettre un chapeau de soleil	(I'm going to put on a sun hat)

Un chapeau de soleil, un chapeau de soleil	
Je vais mettre un chapeau de soleil	
En été.	(in summer)
Je vais danser dans le beau parc	(I'm going to dance in the lovely park)
...Au printemps	(in spring)
Je vais pique-niquer dans les bois	(I'm going to picnic in the wood)
...En automne.	(in autumn)

German

Ich werde einen Schneemann bauen	(I'm going to make a snowman)
einen Schneemann bauen x 2	
Ich werde einen Schneemann bauen	
Im Winter.	(in winter)
Ich werde einen Sonnenhut tragen	(I'm going to wear a sunhat)
einen Sonnenhut tragen x 2	
Ich werde einen Sonnenhut tragen	
Im Sommer.	(in summer)

Ich werde im schönen Park tanzen	(I'm going to dance in the lovely park)
...Im Frühling	(in spring)
Ich werde im Wald Picknick machen	(I'm going to picnic in the wood)
...Im Herbst.	(in autumn)

Classroom instructions

Classroom instructions can work well in song form combined with appropriate actions.

Tune of *Agadoo*

French

Marchez vite, vite, vite	(Walk quickly)
Levez-vous, asseyez-vous	(Stand up, sit down)
Sautez trois fois à gauche	(Jump three times to your left)
Dansez lentement à droite.	(Dance slowly to your right)

German

Geht mal schnell, schnell, schnell	(Walk quickly)
Steht auf, setzt euch	(Stand up, sit down)
Springt dreimal nach links	(Jump three times to your left)
Tanzt langsam nach rechts.	(Dance slowly to your right)

Body parts

Naming body parts and singing greetings make a good partner song, with a wave to your friend.

Tune of *The Animals Went in Two by Two*

French

Touchez la tête et touchez les yeux	(Touch your head and touch your eyes)
Bonjour ! Bonjour !	
Touchez le nez et touchez la bouche	(Touch your nose and touch your mouth)
Bonjour ! Bonjour !	
Touchez le cou et touchez le dos	(Touch your neck and touch your back)
Touchez le bras et touchez l'épaule	(Touch your arm and touch your shoulder)
Un, deux, trois, quatre,	
Bonjour ! Au Revoir !	

German

Berührt den Kopf und auch die Augen	(Touch your head and also your eyes)
Hallo! Hallo!	
Berührt die Nase und auch den Mund	(Touch your nose and also your mouth)
Hallo! Hallo!	
Berührt den Hals und auch den Rücken	(Touch your neck and also your back)
Berührt den Arm und auch die Schulter	(Touch your arm and also your shoulder)
Eins, zwei, drei, vier,	
Hallo! Tschüssi!	

ACTION RHYMES

What other school subject invites everyone to get up in the middle of the lesson, dance around or act like a rocket? We want children's language experience to be meaningful but also memorable, enjoyable and accessible. This approach also gives many opportunities for paired and partner work where communication with others is the key. These examples of action rhymes can be the starting point for a lesson to wake up a class and remind them of the fun in store in the next half hour or so or a reward for great concentration and co-operation. When you make up your own, try to bear in mind the following useful steps:

- use the 'I say, you repeat' format;
- look for repetition or a chorus;
- choose easy memorable actions;
- establish a steady rhythm;
- look for an exciting finale;
- bring in an element of suspense to keep everyone guessing;
- establish a versatile model so that older children do not feel too self-conscious.

If you are not confident about singing, the nearest thing is to make up some action rhymes where children can use a steady rhythm to practise language. Most of the songs suggested above could be converted into a rhyme with a strong beat and suitable actions. For example, for more experienced classes, two lines could face each other for a 'question and answer' format and the first side ask: *Where are you going? Where you going?* with their hands cupping their mouths as if they are calling out. The teacher holds up two cards and the reply might be: *I'm going swimming and I'm going to play tennis* (with an action for each). Then the opposite side ask the question.

Body parts lend themselves well to action rhymes. There is no end to the possibilities of touching parts of your head or your body and calling out numbers or spinning round, marching on the spot or jumping up in the air. Adding a bit of dancing is often a winner as long as you join in, as children love to see teachers looking rather silly. For example:

English
One, two, three, touch your head,
Four, five, six, jump, jump,
Seven, eight, nine, touch your knees,
Ten, ten, ten, turn around.

French
Un, deux, trois, touchez la tête,
Quatre, cinq, six, sautez, sautez !
Sept, huit, neuf, touchez les genoux,
Dix, dix, dix, tournez-vous.

German
Eins, zwei, drei, berührt den Kopf,
Vier, fünf, sechs, springt, springt,
Sieben, acht, neun, berührt die Knie,
Zehn, zehn, zehn, dreht euch herum.

Or:

English
Walk, walk, run, run
Jump, jump, touch your feet
Dance, dance, turn around
One, two, three, four, five.

French
Marchez, marchez, courez, courez,
Sautez, sautez, touchez les pieds,
Dansez, dansez, tournez-vous
Un, deux, trois, quatre, cinq.

German
Geht, geht, lauft, lauft
Springt, springt, berührt die Füße
Tanzt, tanzt, dreht euch herum
Eins, zwei, drei, vier, fünf.

End on a star jump!

You could turn these into clapping rhymes where children clap routines in pairs or even standing in lines, tapping on each other's backs. Another possibility is to incorporate them into skipping rhymes for the playground; they make an intriguing attraction for bystanders.

Teddy Bear Rhyme

This is a good starter for beginners who have learned a few classroom instructions. Start with everyone sitting facing the teacher, hanging heads like sleeping teddy bears. As you say the instructions they copy the words and do the actions:

French

Nounours	Teddy Bear
Nounours, nounours levez-vous !	(Get up!)
Nounours, nounours tournez-vous !	(Turn round)
Nounours, nounours dîtes 'bonjour' !	(Wave hand, say 'hello')
Nounours, nounours asseyez-vous !	(Sit down)
Nounours, nounours dormez bien.	(Hang head, go back to sleep)

German

Teddybär	
Teddy, Teddy, steh auf!	(Get up!)
Teddy, Teddy, dreh dich herum!	(Turn round)
Teddy, Teddy, sag 'Hallo'!	(Wave hand, say 'hello')
Teddy, Teddy, setz dich	(Sit down)
Teddy, Teddy schlaf gut!	(Hang head, go back to sleep)

The Rocket

This is a simple but exciting way to practise numbers and to have a little performance. Even children who know their numbers need to practise saying them in reverse. You could demonstrate this first and then let them guess what the rhyme is about. Tantalise them by delaying saying the 'zero' so they have to wait for the excitement. Everyone works in unison. Play a 'beat the teacher' game to catch them out, for example the children look around, you call the title to surprise them and see if they can be ready before you!

Vocabulary: numbers in reverse from ten to zero.

French
dix, neuf, huit, sept, six, cinq, quatre, trois, deux, un, zéro

German
zehn, neun, acht, sieben, sechs, fünf, vier, drei, zwei, eins, null

Steps:

1 Call out *The rocket* (in **French** *La fusée* in **German** *Die Rakete*).
2 Stand absolutely still and put your hands together in front of you as if in prayer. Insist on silence and complete attention.
3 Count down from *ten* to *five* slowly, with students repeating after you. Keep your hands still. When you reach *five*, move your hands slightly upwards, still together. When you get to *zero*, call that number loudly all together, bringing your hands up and then down by your sides as if for a rocket taking off. You could play it again with a volunteer calling out the numbers or a group taking it in turns.

To the Left, To the Right
This action rhyme can be taught in the first term and still be useful a couple of years later as a reminder and a short lesson filler. Teach it line by line, with the class repeating. Do it first with the class facing you to learn the steps and then they can perform in pairs facing one another. Children love it as a moving game and you can perform it several times in succession. They can change partners each time you complete the rhyme as you call out *One, two, three, CHANGE!* (**French:** *Un, deux, trois, CHANGEZ !* **German:** *Eins, zwei, drei, Plätze tauschen!*) and *to the left, to the right* (**French:** *à gauche, à droite*, **German:** *links, rechts*).

Steps:

Follow these actions in order:

English: left, right	**Action:** stretch both arms in each direction to the side

French: à gauche, à droite x 2

German: links, rechts x 2

English: up, down	**Action:** raise and lower both arms

French: en haut, en bas x 2

German: auf, ab x 2

English: in front, behind	**Action:** arms in front and then behind heads

French: en avant, en arrière x 2

German: nach vorn, nach hinten x2

English: slowly, slowly	**Action:** slowly raise arms in front and then lower them

French: lentement, lentement x 2

German: langsam, langsam x 2

(Keep them waiting in suspense here as this next bit is a favourite!)

English: quickly, quickly	**Action:** quickly move arms up and down

French: vite, vite x 2

German: schnell, schnell x 2

English: great, great! **Action:** both thumbs up in front of them in triumph

French: génial, génial ! x 2

German: toll, toll! x 2

The Week

Make a collection of simple verbs which describe an action you might practise at school, in physical education or in the classroom. Discuss which actions you might perform on different days. Look for an interesting culmination to the week for Sunday. Use a steady rhythm. Everyone repeats after you and does an action for each verb. Have a dramatic action for the final line as in the example below.

English: The week	French: La semaine	German: Die Woche
On Monday I sleep	Lundi je dors	Am Montag schlafe ich
On Tuesday I run	Mardi je cours	Am Dienstag laufe ich
On Wednesday I walk	Mercredi je marche	Am Mittwoch spaziere ich
On Thursday I jump	Jeudi je saute	Am Donnerstag springe ich
On Friday I swim	Vendredi je nage	Am Freitag schwimme ich
On Saturday I read	Samedi je lis	Am Samstag lese ich
and on Sunday I dance!	et dimanche je danse !	und am Sonntag tanze ich!

To make a more complicated rhyme, replace the verbs above by making a list together of hobbies or activities which students like doing, for example: *I play football; I do sport; I listen to music; I play the violin.*

French
je joue au foot; je fais du sport; j'écoute de la musique; je joue du violon.

German
ich spiele Fußball; ich treibe Sport; ich höre Musik; ich spiele Geige.

In pairs, students could make up their own rhyme and perform it with a partner, using an appropriate action for each phrase. They could announce the title: *Hannah's week; la semaine de Hannah; Hannahs Woche* etc.

The Rainbow
This is an easy rhyme for beginners in their first term using some common colours, although they are not the authentic colours of the rainbow of course! Have a set of colour flashcards for volunteers to hold up.

Steps:

• Call out a colour name and choose a child to come to the front of the class to hold the card.
• Select about six or seven colours, as far as possible the colours of the rainbow.
• You say each line of the rhyme, they repeat and a child raises that colour card.
• On the last line, each person raises their card in turn to make the arc shape and everyone else slowly moves both their arms in the air from one side to the other to represent the arc and calls out the final words together.

English: the rainbow	French: l'arc-en-ciel	German: der Regenbogen
Here's the blue	Voici le bleu	Hier ist das Blau
Here's the red	Voici le rouge	Hier ist das Rot
Here's the yellow	Voici le jaune	Hier ist das Gelb
Here's the green	Voici le vert	Hier ist das Grün
Here's the purple	Voici le violet	Hier ist das Violett
Here's the pink	Voici le rose	Hier ist das Rosa
Here's the orange	Voici l'orange	Hier ist das Orange
And there it is; the rainbow!	Et voilà ! L'arc-en-ciel !	Und hier ist er; der Regenbogen!

CHAPTER 7
Exploring Stories

One of the best parts of being a primary school teacher has to be the cosy time when you gather the whole class tightly around you, shut the door to the outside world, lower your voice and share a story. Our favourites have always been on gloomy winter afternoons with a candle in a lantern nearby (Risk Assessments duly filled in!) and the soft, flickering glow lighting up your page. Luckily stories come in all sorts of shapes and sizes and even in other languages! This chapter collects together some easily transferable ideas and suggestions to help you try out stories, poems and rhymes with your class and bring your reading material to life.

When you have explored a topic and feel on top of the vocabulary, try to find a simple text which will bring an extra dimension to your language learning. It makes sense to use a story which reflects the topic you have been exploring so that the children feel confident about looking at whole sentences, enjoy being word detectives and deciphering a scaffolded text. You are not aiming for the children to understand every word of a story but to get the gist, recognise and respond to key words, notice some phonic patterns, pick up some of the intonation and shape of the language and to appreciate that stories are an important part of cultural life all over the world.

CHOOSING A TEXT

One of the problems is to find a story at the right intellectual level for your class, but which matches their language ability. You will know your class and can anticipate whether they will turn their noses up at a familiar cosy story for young children or a traditional tale. In our experience, most classes will cheerfully and somewhat nostalgically enjoy revisiting modern, childhood classics and will find the familiarity of the story helpful. They, in a strange way, become the experts about the story and are happy to rediscover the plot in another language.

Look for short, engaging texts which contain a repetitive phrase which children can recite in unison. If possible, find a version with pictures which can provide clues for understanding new vocabulary. Remember that learning to read in another language has many similarities to learning to read in your native language. As a primary school teacher you will be familiar with all those strategies – sounding out words using phonic skills, using picture clues, using prior knowledge, using context to work out meaning.

INTRODUCING THE STORY

Single out some key words to teach first; perhaps character names, the repeated phrase, maybe the introductory equivalent of *Once upon a time…* (**French:** *il était une fois…*; German: *es war einmal…*) and point out any vocabulary which you know that your class have been learning and is the reason why you have selected this particular story. Examples could be: food words; clothes words; phrases to say *I love…* and *I hate….*

To involve children more fully, you could prepare little cards with pictures of the main characters on them or key words. Distribute them amongst the class and ask them to wave them in the air when they hear their character name or key word. When you approach the section with the repeated phrase, have a prepared signal so that the class are ready to join in, using an appropriate tone of voice.

If you are reading a story in the very early stages of language learning, you will probably read it like a story session at the end of the school day, without showing the text but still expecting the class to join in at the prepared stages. With more experienced groups you may decide to read the story first without showing the text, asking the class to listen to the shape and sound of the language and see what they recognise. Most classes will enjoy listening intently, perhaps raising a finger discreetly to indicate a familiar phrase they have noticed. Then display the text, if possible on a large whiteboard, and read it again, following the guidelines you've practised. Encourage everyone to join in the repeated phrases in an overly dramatic way (children are very resourceful about inventing mimes and actions to embellish the experience) and try to keep the pace lively.

PHONICS

When you have read and explored the story fully, look out for any phonic repetition, such as the use of *oi* in French as in *trois, moi, bois*. Practise it and invite children to look for other examples in the text. Encourage them to search for other phonic patterns, discuss their similarities and differences to English and use them in a display in the classroom, perhaps hanging from hoops from the ceiling so that children can try them out as they move about each day. Children are always keen to spot new examples and then work out a rule for pronouncing phonemes or spotting silent letters.

RECOMMENDATIONS

One of the most popular and successful books used in Primary Languages has been *Va-t'en, Grand Monstre Vert* by Ed Emberley (2012). Its success is due to its brilliant bold pictures of a monster being assembled in its different parts, the accessible and useful language (colours, parts of the face, *go away*) and its sheer exuberance. It makes a versatile vehicle for teaching any of those subjects, with a repeated phrase for a chorus, and is ideal for adapting for an assembly with a group performing as the monster and the class as the chorus. The animal books *Ours brun, dis-moi...* (Martin and Carle, 2001) and *Ours blanc, dis-moi...* (Carle, 2013) also have a simple format with lots of repetition based on animals and colours and lend themselves to chanting in a two-part chorus. The familiar story *Dear Zoo* by Rod Campbell (1982) has been popular too in European languages, with a focus on animals and adjectives, a repeated phrase and a cosy appealing story.

MOVING ON

The story can be revisited several times over different lessons as children develop more proficiency. It could be used as an example in an assembly or as a mini-event to show parents how stories in foreign languages are used (See also Chapter 8, 'Showing the World') and also as a teaching sequence to show your less experienced colleagues how to approach the rather daunting task of using a text in another language. The story could also eventually form the basis of a little play (see for example the story of *The Three Little Pigs* later in this chapter) which the class could act out, with a confident child or group of children as the narrator, the whole class calling out the repeated phrases and individuals as the main characters. Record it on a DVD and use it to show visitors or inspectors as evidence of a structured piece of language learning. You can also use the text as a springboard for a wide variety of other activities. Here are some ideas.

What's Missing?
This can be a quick activity based on the text and can be adapted for any level of understanding. Reproduce short phrases or sentences from the story with key words concealed by sticky notes. Children guess what is missing and identify what kind of word class it is, for example a verb or a noun.

Quick Change
Extract a simple sentence from the story and identify its components. This example comes from *Ours brun, dis-moi...*:

Ours brun, ours brun, dis-moi ce que tu vois.

In this case *ours brun* (*brown bear*) is a noun with its colour adjective placed after the noun. *Dis-moi* (*tell me*) is a verb in the imperative or command form with a pronoun attached. *Ce que* (*what*) is a connective joining up the two parts of the sentence, whilst *tu vois* (*you see*) is a verb with its pronoun.

You could then change some part of the sentence to create a scaffold which children can adapt. Younger children could keep to a change of animal and colour whereas older children could attempt a more radical change. For example, they could exhange *ours brun* for a different animal or person. Similarly, with some help with compiling a list of verbs, they could exchange *tu vois* for another verb in the *tu* form. Thus, you can develop sentences such as: *oiseau bleu, oiseau bleu, dis-moi ce que tu vois* or *ours brun, ours brun, dis-moi ce que tu manges.* You could change both into something like: *chien blanc, chien blanc, dis-moi ce que tu bois.* Children could then explore their own animal and what it can do/see/hear/eat/touch etc.

Human Sentence

This is one of the most popular sentence-level games and is easy to manage at all stages of learning. It is definitely one for children to get up and do rather than carry out on a whiteboard as the physical element is all-important. Choose a useful sentence from the story, print out the separate words (and any punctuation) in large font size onto cards, jumble them up and invite volunteers to hold them in a random order at the front of the classroom. Read aloud together the jumbled mix and then ask the volunteers to rearrange themselves in the correct order. Read aloud again and invite comments about how they worked it out, inviting suggestions for any alternative order. Next, keep reading aloud several times in unison as the teacher gradually turns each card over to the blank side. The children keep reciting the sentence until there are no words visible and they are reading from memory. Children tend to think this is some sort of magic trick, but it is very useful for developing memory and analysing sentence structures.

Mixed Up

Identify a section of the story which has several shortish sentences and can be complete in itself. If you have a whiteboard, jumble up the sentences and ask the class to re-order them as you read the passage. Alternatively, type out the section, photocopy it and cut it into separate sentences. Give each group or pair an envelope containing the sentences and ask them to place them in order as you read the passage. Read aloud the corrected order together several times in different voices.

Next the teacher reads aloud from the complete sentences and stops at different places. Each time s/he stops, the children read the next word in the sequence and then the process begins again. More experienced children may enjoy the challenge of this next extension. Ask the class to remove or turn over one sentence, but still recite it out loud in its place. Continue with the other sentences until there are none in view, but the whole passage can still be recited.

Little Dictation
If your class have enjoyed the challenge of the previous activity, try out a little dictation. This used to be one of the staples of language teaching and is an excellent exercise in listening and applying logic and grammar rules. Simply read one of the sentences from the passage slowly, repeating each phrase twice, while the class try to write down what you say and then check it together. Try to keep this light and accessible; this is an area where practice makes a big difference.

Magnetic Words
This game reminds us of the magnetic words you can put on your fridge and rearrange in different ways. Rather like 'Mixed Up' above, take a sentence with a recognisable verb, noun, and adjective from the story you've been reading and separate all the words so they are completely spread out on the whiteboard or on paper in front of each group or table. For younger children keep the mix predictable and familiar and then add more when they are ready. Older children might manage some extra words added to the mix which have the same function as existing words, for example, extra adjectives, alternative nouns and verbs in the same person. It is also handy to add *and* to extend the sentences. Challenge the class to make up as many different sentences as possible using the words available and the format from the passage, with bonus

points to anyone who can extend their sentence with *and*. They could make a note of their findings on a mini-whiteboard. If they respond well to this, give them other connectives such as *but* and *because*. When they become proficient, you could always use this as a two-minute starter to the lesson or a quick plenary.

More games and activities to use with stories can be found after the German playlet on page 137. Although the examples given are based on the German text, the ideas can be transferred easily to French or any other language.

SUITABLE TEXTS

There are a variety of picture books available in European languages which lend themselves to the usual topics taught in primary schools, many of which can be bought online via www.littlelinguist.co.uk. You will recognise many of the language books available in French and German as the majority of them are familiar picture stories originally written in English like *The Very Hungry Caterpillar* (Carle, 1969), *Elmer* (McKee, 1989), *We're Going on a Bear Hunt* (Rosen, 1989). A good range of items can also be sourced from the internet, often accompanied by audio and video clips, thereby extending the boundaries of your own teaching model. A useful website in this context is: http://uk.mantralingua.com/ which has a range of teaching resources and, in particular, foreign language storybooks for the primary classroom. Try to check the text before buying to make sure that it will be accessible for your age group. The best way by far to do this is to have a trip to a bookshop with a wide supply of these books and treat yourself to a browsing session, but of course this is not always possible.

TELLING STORIES

This section is based around a well-known fairy tale in German (*The Three Little Pigs*), which is easy to adapt to other languages. The tale, presented here as a playlet, is explored in detail through a range of different activity types, as dealing with a whole story together in a foreign language is demanding even if your class knows the basic outline of the story, and needs to be approached gradually. Thus, one story may well take several sessions to explore, enabling you to build depth to the activities and possibly culminating in a whole-class performance for a school assembly (see also Chapter 8, 'Showing the World').

The Three Little Pigs
Many primary school children are familiar with this tale about three piglets who build different houses and are chased by the big, bad wolf. It is a simple story with lots of repetition and lends itself well to whole-class performance as everyone can have a part, be it a wolf, a pig, a house or a part in the chorus. Here is the story in German, which is followed by a range of different, transferable activities. It is worth looking at Project Five in Part Five of *Living Languages: An Integrated Approach to Teaching Foreign Languages in Primary Schools* (Watts, Forder and Phillips, 2013), which contains full details about how to adapt a story to make a playscript.

Resources: the seven pictures in Figure 7.1, laminated and stuck onto lollipop sticks; dungarees and stripy T-shirts for the pigs to wear; spotted handkerchiefs on sticks for the pigs to carry along the way; a tail and a top hat for the wolf to wear; the words for the chorus to display; identical outfits for the narrators to wear if you have more than one.

Figure 7.1 The Three Little Pigs

PLAYSCRIPT OF *THE THREE LITTLE PIGS*

By Cathy Watts

Narrator: Es waren einmal drei kleine Schweinchen.

Piglet 1: Ich bin das erste Schwein.

Piglet 2: Ich bin das zweite Schwein.

Piglet 3: Und ich bin das dritte Schwein

Narrator: Jedes Schweinchen baute sich ein Haus.

Piglet 1: Mein Haus ist aus Stroh (*points to house i.e. two children forming an arch and one child holding up the picture*).

Piglet 2: Mein Haus ist aus Holz (*points to house i.e. two children forming an arch and one child holding up the picture*).

Piglet 3: Und mein Haus ist aus Stein (*points to house i.e. two children forming an arch and one child holding up the picture*).

Narrator: Im Wald lebte der böse Wolf.

Wolf: Ich bin der Wolf. Ich bin sehr böse (*spoken with a deep, growly voice*). Ich bin auch sehr hungrig (*the three pigs squeak with terror*).

Narrator: Der Wolf ging zum ersten Haus.

Wolf: Liebes, gutes Schwein, lass mich doch zu dir hinein!

Piglet 1: Nein!! (*stamps foot*).

Wolf (*and chorus of children*): Dann huste ich und puste ich, bis dein Haus kaputt ist! (*children forming bridge for first house fall on the floor*).

Narrator: Das Schweinchen läuft in das Haus seines Bruders (*first piglet runs to second house made by the bridge of children*).

Narrator: Nun geht der Wolf zum Holzhaus.

Wolf: Liebes, gutes Schwein, lass mich doch zu dir hinein.

Piglet 2: Nein!! (*makes a fist*).

Wolf (*and chorus of children*): Dann huste ich und puste ich, bis dein Haus kaputt ist! (*children forming bridge for second house fall on the floor*).

Narrator: Die zwei Schweinchen laufen zum dritten Haus (*first piglet and second piglet run to third house made by the bridge of children*).

Wolf (*knocks on door of house made of stone*): Liebes, gutes Schwein, lass mich doch zu dir hinein.

Piglet 3: Nein!! (*makes a fist and stamps foot. The two other pigs shake and tremble in the background*).

Wolf (*and chorus of children*): Dann huste ich und puste ich, bis dein Haus kaputt ist!

Narrator: Und er hustet und er pustet aber das Haus geht nicht kaputt. Er klettert auf das Dach (*Wolf climbs up on top of the bridge of children using a chair*) und durch den Schornstein (*Wolf falls through the arch of children*) und fällt ins Feuer. Nun rennt er schnell davon (*Wolf runs away holding his bottom and howling*).

Narrator: Jetzt waren die drei Schweinchen wieder glücklich (*three pigs dance for joy*).

Whole class together: Und wenn sie nicht gestorben sind, dann leben sie noch heute!

Working with words
Individual words in stories are not always easy to grasp, as they are often story-specific and not used so much out of context. Key words in the text you choose need to be isolated and pre-taught to help the children make sense of the story. In the 'Three Little Pigs' story, these are the key words which the class need to understand before they hear the tale:

das Schwein: pig (cf. swine)	*das Schweinchen*: piglet
der Wolf: wolf	*das Haus*: house
das Haus aus...: the house made of...	*das Stroh*: straw
das Holz: wood	*der Stein*: stone
der/ die/ das erste...: the first/ second/ third...	*das Feuer*: fire
der Bruder: brother	*das Dach*: roof
der Wald: wood	*der Schornstein*: chimney

Interestingly, the words in German and English are very similar in many cases, making it easier for the children to try to guess the meaning of individual items in the first instance. You can use the pictures provided to add a visual dimension to the text by asking the children to link them to the key words.

Repetition
Ask the class to repeat each word after you, following your pronunciation model. The children can say the words aloud or under their breath, putting their hands up when they are ready to speak, and focusing on their own pronunciation.

You can mouth the words as well without making a sound. Can the children recognise what the word is just by looking at your mouth? Can they imitate your model themselves?

As the class become more confident with the story, they can join in a chorus together such as:

> *Liebes, gutes Schwein, lass mich doch zu dir hinein.*
> (Dear, good piglet do let me come in.)

139

and

> *Dann huste ich und puste ich, bis dein Haus kaputt ist!*
> (Then I'll huff and I'll puff until your house is broken!)

Try saying the chorus lines together in different voices. For example, you could be sad, angry, happy or shy and use your intonation to convey these feelings, as well as gestures and body language. Try different volume levels too, for example you could whisper, or encourage everyone to roar out like a big, bad wolf. The louder the better! In this way children develop confidence with the target language and a great sense of enjoyment and fun is stimulated.

Why not add your own sound effects too? In the story above, for example, the wolf's actions could be accompanied by growling noises each time, which could lead to further work on the noises made by different animals in the foreign language.

Actions too can be an effective accompaniment to your story, as the children show they understand and recognise specific words and phrases using a physical response. Thus, a round of huffing and blowing after the wolf has said his lines might fit in well and the children could wave goodbye to the pigs each time one of them moves house!

FURTHER IDEAS AND GAMES TO USE WITH A TEXT

Word segments

Once the key vocabulary is familiar, you can cut the longer individual words in half and ask the class to put them back together again. To help embed the word patterns, you could ask your children in groups to organise a pile of individual letters into the correct words – and then organise the completed words into dictionary order, i.e. each child stands in order according to the first letter of the word, as in: *Bruder; Dach; Feuer; Haus; Holz; Schornstein Schwein; Schweinchen; Stein; Stroh; Wald; Wolf.*

You could play a syllable clapping game too, which will help embed new vocabulary and give everyone the chance to get a feel for the language in terms of the way it is pronounced. This is a simple technique: you clap out the syllables in the words (one clap for each syllable) and the children guess which word you have chosen. Thus, *Schornstein* becomes *Schorn-stein* (two claps). Can the children do this too in groups?

Similarities and differences

It is interesting how many words in the target language are very similar to their English counterparts. You could use your story to notice similarities and differences between words in the target language and English and encourage your class to recognise that languages borrow words from each other. This practice also encourages children to use what they know about their own language to help them learn a new one. In the context of *The Three Little Pigs*, the topic of similarities between animals is appropriate and fun to look at together.

das Schwein: pig (cf. swine)	*die Giraffe*: giraffe
der Wolf: wolf	*die Maus*: mouse
die Katze: cat	*der Hund*: dog (cf. hound)
der Tiger: tiger	*der Fuchs*: fox
der Bär: bear	*der Frosch*: frog

Sentences 1

You can encourage your class to recognise the type of text they are dealing with by looking at the beginning and end of the piece of writing. Fairy tales in many languages start and finish with specific words. In English, for example, they normally start with *Once upon a time...* and end with *...and they all lived happily ever after*. The German story above starts with the phrase *Es waren einmal...* and ends with *...und wenn sie nicht gestorben sind, dann* *leben sie noch heute.* Practise saying the German endings with your class, as they can transfer this information to other stories at a later date. You could practise these sentences by playing the game *Where am I?* This involves displaying a familiar sentence or string of words from your story for everyone to see. Read the sentence aloud, but stop along the way at different points and ask the class to say the next word in the sequence.

Reading aloud

Reading your text aloud helps foster links between the spoken and the written word. You can either use your own voice as the model for the children to follow, or source CDs and videos on the internet spoken by native speakers. Many teachers like to use finger puppets to illustrate the story (see also Chapter 5, 'Being Creative' for how to make finger puppets out of rubber gloves). If you read the story yourself, you can use a variety of voices and expressions, as well as any pictures, to tell the story slowly and clearly whilst your class listens quietly (unless they join in with the chorus parts). Some of the verbs the children will not know, but you can mime these or make gestures to explain them. For example, the verb *klettern* (to climb) can be demonstrated with two fingers climbing up just like the wolf on the roof, as can the verb *laufen* (to run) with your two fingers running along the page perhaps.

Letters

It is interesting to focus on the alphabet and letters which are different or similar to those in English. You can ask your class to make a list of letters which are different to the English letters they are used to. Examples from *The Three Little Pigs* involve an Umlaut, which has the effect of 'pinching' the sound: ö (as in *böse*); ä (as in *läuft* and *fällt*).

How are letters pronounced in the target language? There are two alphabets at the back of this book to help you practise as a class in French and German (see Appendix 1).

Pass the Anagram Parcel

This game is good fun to play! The children sit in a circle and pass a bag to each other in turn containing letter cards. Music is played (preferably from the target country) and, when this stops, the child holding the bag at that moment withdraws a letter card, identifies it by name and puts it in the middle of the circle. The music restarts and the game continues until all the letters are in the middle of the circle. The children then make words from the letters in the centre.

Pass the Word Parcel

This game is a variation on 'Pass the Anagram Parcel' above and equally good fun to play. In this game, the children sit in a circle and pass a bag amongst themselves, this time containing word cards. Music is played (again preferably from the target country) and, when this stops, the child holding the bag at that moment withdraws a word card and reads it aloud. The other children echo the word, pronunciation is corrected if necessary, the word card is placed in the middle of the circle and the game resumes. Afterwards, the words can be sorted into dictionary order or perhaps into different categories, such as adjectives, nouns, verbs etc.

Sentences 2

Through stories and other texts, children recognise that the order of words in a sentence influences meaning. There are several effective ways to help your class manipulate language effectively, using the story as a basis. At the simplest level, selected sentences from the story can be cut in half. Each small group of children is given a selection of these and asked to put them back together again in the correct order. You could also reproduce some of the text as a gapfill exercise and complete the missing words together. The focus could be on same-word classes, for example all the adjectives or nouns representing materials or parts of a house in *The Three Little Pigs*. Or you could choose to focus on grammatical structures such as question forms, statements or negatives.

Using models based on the story, your class can build up small conversations along the lines of words spoken by the characters in the tale. Here is an example from *The Three Little Pigs*:

143

Question	Answer
Guten Morgen.	Guten Morgen.
Wer bist du?	Ich bin das erste Schwein.
Wie alt bist du?	Ich bin acht Jahre alt.
Wo wohnst du?	Ich wohne mit meinem Bruder.
Was trägst du?	Ich trage… (display items in spotted handkerchief, for example food)

It is always fun to extend such descriptions to the children in your class. The children have to guess who is being described.

English	French	German
She is (nine years old).	Elle a (neuf ans).	Sie ist (neun Jahre alt).
He lives in…	Il habite à…	Er wohnt in…
He is (quite) tall.	Il est (assez) grand.	Er ist (ziemlich) groß.
He has brown/blond hair.	Il a les cheveux bruns/blonds.	Er hat braune/blonde Haare.
She wears glasses.	Elle porte des lunettes.	Sie trägt eine Brille.

Points to notice are the position of adjectives in the sentence (mainly after nouns in French but before them in German) and also the agreement of the adjective with the noun.

Reading for gist
Simple questions and answers in the target language are needed to ensure the children have understood the gist of the story. These may revolve around the number of characters in the story, for example in *The Three Little Pigs* you could ask: *Wie viele*

Charaktere sind in der Geschichte? The answer would be: *Es gibt einen Wolf, einen Narrator und drei Schweinchen.*

Reading for detail
More detailed questions can follow the focus on gist. These can be in English with English answers expected. Some examples of straightforward questions from *The Three Little Pigs* follow, but other question types such as True/False etc. are also appropriate.

1 How many pigs are there?
2 Where do they each live?
3 What are the piglets carrying?
4 Where does the wolf live?
5 How does the wolf get into the third piglet's house?
6 What happens to the wolf in the end?
7 What do the piglets do to celebrate?

The internet contains a wealth of stories in French and German. It is often a question of spending time browsing. Here are just three websites which we have found to be very useful:

1 www.jackhunt.peterborough.sch.uk/page/?title=French+ Primary+Resources&pid=162
2 A selection of French stories: http://chezlorry.ca/histoires.htm
3 Information about the Brothers Grimm and German fairy tales: www.ukgermanconnection.org/kids-stories-songs

READING POEMS

Poems are also an important aspect of primary literacy lessons and combining these with foreign language learning can be enjoyable and fun. As well as the activities outlined above, poems are often short enough to be learnt by heart and presented in a whole-class assembly, perhaps complete with props (see also Chapter 8, 'Showing the World').

Books of poems suitable for young language learners can be found from www.little-linguist.co.uk or www.amazon.fr for French books and www.amazon.de for German resources. These collections are aimed at young native speakers but contain a wealth of very accessible short rhymes and poems (no more than ten short lines with lots of repetition and simple vocabulary) which could be read together with actions and then used as a scaffold for a class poem. Another useful and cheap source of poems is in children's comics or magazines for native speakers which you might pick up in any newsagent abroad. They often contain little dot-to-dot pages, funny poems or puzzles, which you could use in class.

KEY WORD IDENTIFICATION

Your class can make their own finger puppets which they can hold up when they hear a key word read out (see also Chapter 5, 'Being Creative'). This is a very visible and effective way of checking comprehension. If you make up your own poems with your class, you will be able to tailor the words to suit the topic you are covering or need to revise. A poem does not necessarily need to rhyme and can be very flexible in its format. 'The Chameleon', by Cathy Watts, was written to explore colours and habitats and works well with finger puppets made from paper, coloured in and glued onto lollipop sticks.

This short poem is about a chameleon which lives in various places according to what colour it chooses to be! A list of various habitats is included in Chapter 9, 'Starting to Write' ('Writing a half-and-half book'), and here are some useful colours you could use:

English: pink; yellow; brown; silver; blue; green; black

French: rose; jaune; brun; argent; bleu; vert; noir

German: rosa; gelb; braun; silber; blau; grün; schwarz

Resources: a coloured chameleon for each child and seven coloured habitat pictures; a wooden lollipop stick for everyone.

Figure 7.2 A Chameleon Puppet

Steps:

1 The children colour the chameleon in one solid colour which appears in the poem. Seven children colour the different habitats.
2 Glue all the pictures onto lollipop sticks for the children to hold up during the poem.
3 Read the poem aloud slowly. Ask the children to hold up their picture when they hear the word that matches it.

English version

Charles the chameleon: where do you live?

I am pink. I live in the flowers.
I am yellow. I live on the beach.
I am brown. I live on the farm.
I am silver. I live in the air.
I am blue. I live in the sea.
I am green. I live in the forest.
I am black. I live underground.

147

French version

Claude le caméléon: où habites-tu?

Je suis rose. J'habite dans les fleurs.
Je suis jaune. J'habite au bord de la mer.
Je suis brun. J'habite à la ferme.
Je suis argent. J'habite dans l'air.
Je suis bleu. J'habite dans la mer.
Je suis vert. J'habite dans la forêt.
Je suis noir. J'habite sous la terre.

German version

Claus das Chamäleon: wo lebst du?

Ich bin rosa. Ich lebe in den Blumen.
Ich bin gelb. Ich lebe am Strand.
Ich bin braun. Ich lebe auf dem Bauernhof.
Ich bin silber. Ich lebe in der Luft.
Ich bin blau. Ich lebe im Meer.
Ich bin grün. Ich lebe im Wald.
Ich bin schwarz. Ich lebe unter der Erde.

There are several activities you can do with a simple poem like this one. You can try adding one word and joining the two sentences together. For example, if you add the word *and* you'll have one longer sentence as in:

Je suis vert **et** j'habite dans la forêt.

Ich bin grün **und** ich lebe im Wald.

An alternative is to focus on different constructions such as negative sentences as in:

Je suis vert. Je **n**'habite **pas** dans la mer.

Ich bin grün. Ich lebe **nicht** im Meer.

You could practise questions and answers in small groups as in:

English	French	German
What colour are you?	Tu es de quelle couleur?	Welche Farbe bist du?
I am (brown).	Je suis (brun).	Ich bin (braun).
Where do you live?	Où habites-tu?	Wo lebst du?
I live (on the farm).	J'habite (à la ferme).	Ich lebe auf dem Bauernhof.

It is fun if the children use the stick puppets they have made to answer the questions. In Chapter 5, 'Being Creative' there are some suggestions for making different types of puppets ('Rubber glove people'). Alternatively, you could encourage your class to make paper finger puppets from an online source such as: www.ukgermanconnection.org/kids-mrpunch-fingerpuppen or www.ukgermanconnection.org/kids-make-stadtmusikanten-puppets. Making paper masks too can really bring your story to life. An inspiring website is: www.teachingzone.org/topics/topics_masks.htm.

CULTURAL INFORMATION

Poems are often an effective way into cultural information, as they are part of the traditions of the country / countries where the target language is spoken. Here are two texts which were written to celebrate Christmas and they lend themselves well to further exploration in the context of this topic. The following short verse in German is said by German children to Saint Nikolaus when he comes to them on Nikolaustag (December 6th). Saint Nikolaus is traditionally accompanied by Knecht Ruprecht with his bundle of birch twigs (*eine Rute*). If the children have been good, they get presents from Santa. If they have been naughty, they get a hiding!

Father Christmas	**Der Weihnachtsmann**
My dear Father Christmas	Lieber guter Weihnachtsmann
Don't look at me so angrily.	sieh mich nicht so böse an.
Please put away your switch/sticks	Stecke deine Rute ein,
And I'll be good for ever after!	will auch immer artig sein!

In French, Saint-Nicolas also has a partner, le Père Fouettard (Father Spanker) whose job it is to decide whether children have been good or bad. If the latter, he dishes out a spanking! Still on a Christmas theme, you could use a traditional carol (or part of one) like a poem. This traditional one in French, *Vive le vent*, has the same tune as *Jingle bells*. The first verse could be accompanied by the children blowing hard like a sharp wind as you read it aloud. And of course, it makes a good link with a (winter) weather topic too!

Long Live the Wind

Long live the wind, long live the wind, long live the wind of winter
Which goes about whistling and blowing
In the tall, green pine trees. Oh!
Long live the wind, long live the wind, long live the wind of winter.

Vive le vent

Vive le vent, vive le vent, vive le vent d'hiver
Qui s'en va, sifflant, soufflant
Dans les grands sapins verts,
Oh ! Vive le vent, vive le vent, vive le vent d'hiver.

DEALING WITH NON-FICTION TEXTS

As children increase their understanding of the target language, they gain confidence in dealing with different text types in paper and electronic forms, such as, invitations, e-mails, letters, information texts, advertisements, recipes, letters, messages and so on. Often authentic texts have similar conventions to their English counterparts and, by noticing these with your class, you raise awareness of written conventions in the target language. This is an opportunity to investigate Our Word Collections where your class could put together any street phrases they may have spotted in cafés, trains, shops etc. from their holiday trips (see Chapter 1, 'Setting the Scene'). What can they work out from just a few clues? Children can learn to recognise non-fiction texts from their style and layout. For example, a recipe or a street sign is easy to identify from its layout alone, even if the words are not always familiar.

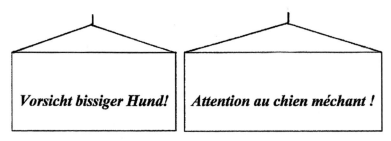

Figure 7.3 Beware of the Dog!

CHAPTER 8

Showing the World

Over the last 10 years, there has been a transformation in language learning in primary schools in the UK and a growing determination that children should start to learn a language from an early age. Part of your role is to show the wider school community some of the skills you are teaching and the enjoyment of the children involved, as well as to demonstrate the methods you employ to enthuse your classes. Try to take every chance to show off the language skills your children are developing and to demonstrate the lively, exciting new methods used with young learners these days. In a school, 'showing the world' may start with your support towards colleagues who are apprehensive about teaching languages and may need reassurance with our mantra: *Do a lot with a little*. If you are a confident language teacher, look for ways to bring more reluctant colleagues along with you, perhaps by team teaching, combining classes for short sessions, demonstrating short routines in a staff meeting, sharing lesson plans. In this chapter, the ideas for assembly presentations may be a stepping stone on this path.

Many parents probably harbour uncomfortable memories of their own stumbling efforts to speak in another language and will be amazed by the sheer joy, enthusiasm and expertise which primary school children can demonstrate after only a few lessons. This chapter considers a variety of ways you can show the world outside your classroom what can be achieved in a foreign language.

SURVEY YOUR SCHOOL COMMUNITY

Look on your own doorstep for colleagues to support you and add their enthusiasm. Your first step may be to discover what hidden talents are held in your school. It is common to meet language co-ordinators who have discovered a fund of knowledge and quiet enthusiasm amongst their colleagues who were otherwise too modest to speak up. Remember to ask office staff and teaching assistants as well, as they can often be key people who are keen to share their interest.

INVOLVING PARENTS

Parents and carers will be your main audience and may also provide expertise of their own and fervent support for the general principle of language learning. You could send out a questionnaire to find out what languages are spoken at home and to ask if parents would be willing to come into school to read a story, sing a song or talk a little about a festival or birthday celebration. Investigate how they might support language work done at school or complement it in a different way, for example by talking about cultural experiences or helping to prepare displays about or food from their country. You may be pleasantly surprised at how enthusiastic parents can be at coming into a classroom and helping out in this way.

Story reading by parents
You may discover a rich resource of language speakers willing to come into school and read a simple story to a class. The wider the range of languages, the more exciting the project could be. Consider setting up monthly or termly story reading sessions where parents prepare a story in advance and rotate around different classes. Bear in mind that parents are sometimes overawed by the prospect of reading to thirty children at once and need some guidelines to help to make the experience meaningful for everyone. Useful guidance would include:

- Choose a story from a book with some pictures to show, perhaps a folk tale.
- Choose a story which is not too long or complicated, even for older pupils.
- Look for repetition or select a character's name from the story so that children can listen for these words.

- Teach the children the repeated words first and explain how the story goes in English.
- Give some of the class (or all of them if possible) a home-made prop such as a tiny coloured flag or feather or picture of fruit to represent something in the story. They will wave this when they hear the key words read from the story.
- Read the story in the target language, showing the pictures, with the class responding by waving props.
- Discuss together what they found out about the country or the moral of the story.
- Perhaps the parent could record their reading onto a CD and lend the book to the class, who could keep it in the Book Corner for a while.
- Take photos of the event to make a display to encourage other parents and to put in a display book near the front entrance to the school to show visitors.

TAKING HOME A LANGUAGE STORY

We are all familiar with the idea of young children taking home a reading book, perhaps from a structured reading scheme or a class bookcase of suitably chosen books. They serve as a daily practice for the emerging reader and as a valuable link between home and school. After many years of organising these exchanges for the children in her class, one of the authors, Hilary, wondered whether it might be possible to do something similar in another language. Of course there are lots of wonderful paperback picture books available in the most familiar European languages, including a good variety of traditional tales and modern children's classics, but it would be expensive to equip a whole class with a range of these stories, let alone a year group or a whole school. There is also the problem of finding the right level of language and maturity for a class and, at the same time, finding something relevant to their learning. In the end Hilary decided to try to make her own as cheaply and as simply as possible, which she could tailor-make to each topic she taught and to the level of understanding of the children. This turned out to be a very popular approach which was easy to manage.

Why would you do it?
It gives children a chance to practise reading a short language book at home at the right level for their learning and based on the topic studied in the classroom. Additionally, it gives parents and even the wider family a chance to share the language learning and to become involved themselves as much or as little as they want. Taking a language book home becomes a good advertisement for learning a language, as children are keen to show off what they can read and even teach their parents a little knowledge!

Making your own book is easy to organise, requiring just a camera, basic IT skills, a bit of imagination and a little time. It fits in well with normal school procedures which you will have in place already, such as checking books are brought back, exchanging new ones and so on. Once you've got the idea in place, it is easy to see how you could extend it, depending on the circumstances of your school. Some extension possibilities are suggested at the end of the next section.

Setting up a language reading scheme: Hilary's story
I started with ideas for the youngest children, thinking of the simple language exchanges they were used to in class and the tactile approach we adopt, often using soft toys and puppets. We had recently been learning greetings and common body parts so I took photos of the two most popular animals I used with the class and set them up in a variety of positions in the classroom environment. I concentrated on the main animal, the teddy bear, placed a big plaster on different parts of his body (for example, his head, ear, back, foot etc.) which the children would recognise and photographed him with the plasters clearly visible. The story then became an introduction to the teddy bear, based on him talking about each of the aches and pains on his body. Then to the rescue came the second animal, in this case a monkey, who kissed him in greeting and made everything better. There were opportunities to say *hello, goodbye, how are you* etc.

The book was then put together with the appropriate photo taking up half of the page and the simple text in bold at the bottom. It consisted of about twelve pages in all. The pages were photocopied and laminated in school and, in order to make the book very cheap to produce, were hole-punched at the side with treasury tags to allow the pages to be turned easily. Of course there are far more sophisticated, ambitious and expensive ways to make a book, but there can be quite a charm in a simple homespun effort too, especially when you are working on a tight budget.

In essence, the text in the book ran something like this:

Hello Teddy, how are you?
I'm not very well. I've got a headache.
I've got an earache.
I've got a backache.
I've got a tummyache.
I've got a footache etc.
Poor Teddy!
Hello Monkey. How are you?
(*After kissing him*) That's better.
Goodbye Monkey.
Goodbye Teddy. See you soon.

The crucial part to this reading book is the next step. It's all very well to send a written text home but what if the child cannot pronounce the words and just reinforces their own mistakes? So you need to record the spoken words being read with expression and slowly enough for children to repeat the words after you before they turn the page. This could be you, the teacher, if you are confident in speaking in the target language, or a native speaker (perhaps a parent at your school?) or maybe a specialist teacher from the local secondary school who would be willing to help you out. Reproduce this on a CD for each laminated story and keep each complete book in a zipped folder to be taken home safely.

Handy hint: Having a bit of humour goes down well in these stories. Children especially loved the kissing part of the first story when there was a kissing noise on the CD!

It is also useful to put a questionnaire in the pack about how the child and family have used the book, what has been useful, could be improved etc. I found the feedback fascinating; some families all had a turn at reading, others invited their extended family to witness the child reading aloud, some insisted on listening in the car on every journey, others at bedtime. This input should help you to develop the scheme to suit other year groups.

Extension
You could develop a peer-reading project across the school by inviting an older age group to come in and read to younger ones in pairs or small groups. The older ones could write a mini-story specifically for the younger ones.

Further adventures of soft toys

1 Introduce a monkey family using words for family members, size words, colours.
2 Say *hello* to lots of different animals, each with a different greeting, for example: *have a good meal, Rabbit; have a good journey, Cat.*
3 Use lots of prepositions and hide animals around the classroom as in a flap book, for example: *Is Teddy under the table? Is Monkey behind the curtain?*
4 Food is always a good source of amusement and this could be Teddy's favourite meals, which might consist of likely or horribly unlikely combinations.
5 Teddy's favourite hobbies, such as Teddy plays tennis, goes skating.
6 Teddy's week using the days of the week and adjectives, as in: *On Tuesday Teddy is tired.*
7 Teddy's clothes, for example: *Teddy is wearing a blue T-shirt and a yellow hat.* Maybe this could turn out like one of those children's favourites where he wears everything the wrong way round or on the wrong part of his body?

However, you will need other sources for stories and the most popular will centre around the children in the class. You could compile stories together in class during the plenary to your lessons and include photos of the children as the basis of the story. As long as the vocabulary is familiar and the CD is available, it should work. Spare copies could be kept in your class library for children to listen to in quiet moments or at the school entrance where visitors have to wait and might tune in for a moment. It all helps to spread the word about what's going on in your school and the value of learning a language. Keep the scheme small-scale to start with and make sure it is manageable. In time you may find you have started a whole new wave of reading in your class, year group or school.

MINI-EVENTS

Invite parents, other classes, visitors or inspectors to mini-events (perhaps at the end of the school day when they come to collect children from school) which might only be ten minutes long: show them some of your games, songs and rhymes and invite them to join in and try out these new ideas at home or in their own classrooms. Emphasise the oracy strand of early learning (speaking and listening) and look for simple ways for the class to practise and say the same phrases as a group, in pairs, as an action rhyme, as a mini-game, as a song, with finger puppets etc. You could invite your visitors to pair up with a child and perform some of these activities with them, hoping that this will promote interest and practice at home. If this proves popular, you could hold a weekly ten-minute slot when you have an 'Open Classroom' for parents to join in a regular sing-song or game.

ASSEMBLIES

There is a familiar tradition of inviting parents and helpers in to see class presentations or assemblies and these provide an opportunity for a longer display of language learning. You could have a themed assembly on your current topic such as clothes, or one rooted in a popular story, for example a fairy tale. You could focus on a topical festival, for example Mardi Gras, or perform something in an unusual format such as in the round. Some tried and tested ideas are outlined below to get you thinking.

Clothes theme assembly

Start with a Fashion Parade. Children in a small group say *hello*, give their name and age, twirl around and explain something very simple that they are wearing, for example: *I am wearing a skirt/ T-shirt*. A separate group comes on each with a hat (or anything that could have lots of different varieties) and describes it, for example: *I'm wearing an Easter hat; sun hat; winter hat; big hat; small hat.* The next group brings items of the same colour, for example blue T-shirts, and say: *my T-shirt is blue dark blue/ navy* etc. Another group could be dressed entirely in one colour. They declare that their favourite colour is blue and give more details. Brave individuals could parade like a model and either they or a partner could list all the clothes being worn.

Next, the whole class could stand in a circle and sing a colour song (see Chapter 6, 'Using Songs', for examples which keep children on their toes) or play 'Fruit salad' with colour words: give each child one of four colours in turn; when their colour is called they run and change places with another person of that colour. Everyone changes place when the word *Rainbow!* is called.

English	French	German
I'm wearing...	Je porte...	Ich trage...
...a sun hat	...un chapeau de soleil	...einen Sonnenhut
...a winter hat	...un chapeau d'hiver	...einen Winterhut
...a big/ small hat	...un grand/ petit chapeau	...einen großen/ kleinen Hut
My T-shirt is blue	Mon t-shirt est bleu	Mein T-Shirt ist blau
dark blue/ navy blue	bleu foncé/ bleu marine	dunkelblau/ marineblau

Songs and rhymes

Another suitable old favourite circle game is *What colour is the hat?* Children sing and skip around the circle with a variety of coloured hats/berets in the middle; someone goes into the middle, picks one up and the circle sings out its colour. Traditional tunes like *Here we Go Round the Mulberry Bush* have a good steady rhythm suitable for simple questions.

An impressive way of presenting material is to arrange the children in a circle facing outwards while they perform a couple of action rhymes or songs. The perennially popular *Heads, shoulders, knees and toes* song works well like this, as each member of the audience has a good view of an individual performer. You could alter this to fit any body parts your class know or change it to the names of clothes being worn. Give it a 'wow factor' by everyone finishing the song with a star jump. If you have an enthusiastic child as a compère, they could encourage the audience to get to their feet and join in a second time.

In-the-round assembly

This is a great favourite, as it takes the audience by surprise and gives each performer close contact with an audience member. Gather the class in a circle in the centre of the hall so that the audience can get in position around them in concentric circles. Adults can always be seated in the back circle on chairs. This assembly could be any combination of parachute games, action rhymes and circle games. There is no need to invent complicated new activities for this performance: the beauty of it is that even simple things look impressive when performed *en masse*. You could alternate a whole circle activity with one half of the circle at a time standing to perform, or use the two halves to act out a Question and Response activity. Another novel format is to have an inner circle and an outer one. This gives a versatile format where each circle can stand and perform separately, or the two circles can face each other to sing/perform in pairs, and third, the outer ring could rotate one partner at a time in a clockwise direction so that they can perform a song or rhyme with a different partner each time.

First, do some whole class starters, such as any greetings songs (see Chapter 6, 'Using Songs') where children face their neighbours in turn and shake hands/kiss cheeks etc. Next, each child faces the back of the person in front and all together clap out a simple clapping rhythm with easy and useful words, for example: *one, two, three, hello; four, five, six, goodbye; how much; please; thank you; goodbye.*

Perform a little finger puppet rhyme to the audience (see examples in Chapter 6, 'Using Songs'). These could be commercial animal puppets or two simply made paper puppets to be held on a finger (see also Chapter 5, 'Being Creative', for some rubber glove puppets). The rhyme could just consist of greetings, saying hello and goodbye, or be a conversation between the two animals.

Parachute games
Parachute games have a magical quality of their own, especially for visitors or parents who may never have seen the colourful canopy used for a game. If you have enough space in your hall, many simple language games can be played such as raising and lowering the parachute, moving from side to side, shaking a ball or rope from one colour to the next, raising the parachute to a part of the body such as the head, shoulders, or stomach, playing 'Fruit salad' (see page 53), running around the outside and into the centre, using quite accessible language. You could look at Chapters 3 and 4 in this book for some ideas; and Project One in the first chapter of *Living Language: An Integrated Approach to Teaching Foreign Languages in Primary Schools* (Watts, Forder and Phillips, 2013) is also about having fun with parachutes in language lessons. Try to finish your games assembly with a quiet activity such as having half or a third of the class at a time lying like spokes of the wheel under the parachute while the others raise and lower the canopy very slowly and chanting softly the equivalent of *gently, gently.*

French: doucement, doucement.

German: ruhig, ruhig.

Mardi Gras festival assembly

Early spring is usually a good time in the school calendar for showing parents what has been achieved over the past couple of terms and even fussy eaters like the idea of a pancake! People often do not realise how widespread the festival of Mardi Gras (i.e, Shrove Tuesday) is, and enjoy the wider cultural celebrations of carnival etc.

All sing a little introductory song to set the scene. This could be as easy as the words for *pancake*, the equivalent of *Enjoy your meal* and *I'm hungry* or *please* and *thank you* in the target language, repeated several times, plus the words *Mardi Gras*. An obvious tune for these words would be *Frère Jacques*, but see also Chapter 6, 'Using Songs', for other suggestions. Vocabulary for this assembly is at the end of this section.

Arrange a group of cooks to show the ingredients and the utensils to the audience, raising the flour, bowl etc. with the rest of the class calling out its name. You could make it more complex by adding quantities such as a litre/fifty grams. Act out making some food, for example showing how to make a pancake, using only the command part of the verbs involved (*pour, mix, cut, whip, cook, eat*) with the overhead whiteboard showing the ingredients to the audience.

Groups of children then come to the front and say how they like their pancake, for example: *I like a pancake with chocolate; I don't like a pancake with lemon* etc. Act out a little scene where several children go into a shop and order their favourite. Have an exchange between the shopkeeper and each customer with a greeting, ordering a pancake, asking how much it will cost, handing over the money, saying *thank you* and *goodbye*.

Sing another little song about different pancakes to the tune *of She'll Be Coming Round the Mountain*. This could be: *I like pancakes with sugar; I don't like pancakes with strawberry jam* etc. In the chorus add a vigorous *Yes it's true!/ No it's false!* with arms raised, and on the final chorus of the last verse ask the class to jump up to sing with their arms raised in the air.

You could have a little class quiz in front of the audience with one half seated to the left of the cooks and the rest to the right. One cook or a narrator could ask the word for an ingredient and a team game could continue. This could use the 'Fly swat' (see p. 61) format where all the words are displayed on large-font cards and a volunteer from each team with a plastic fly swatter (or a ruler) has to whack the correct word as fast as possible (see also Chapter 4, 'On Your Feet', for other games).

A simple story could be narrated where one of the children makes a pancake, using all the vocabulary demonstrated above, and it goes horribly wrong. For instance, instead of flour she uses rice (a group of children stand at the side and tell the audience secretly what it really is) and ends up with a horrible, pre-made, cardboard, floppy mess, with suitable noises of horror! Finish with a food song, which could be from the many examples on commercial CDs or a list of favourite foods sung to *London's burning* or *Agadoo* with *Yes, yes!* or *No, No!* as a chorus.

English	French	German
pancake	la crêpe	der Pfannkuchen
I'm hungry	j'ai faim	Ich habe Hunger
pour, mix	versez, mélangez	gießen, mischen
whip, cut	fouettez, coupez	schlagen, schneiden
cook, eat	faîtes cuire, mangez	kochen, essen
I like...	j'aime...	Ich mag...
eggs, flour, milk	les oeufs, la farine, le lait	die Eier, das Mehl, die Milch
...pancakes with chocolate	...les crêpes au chocolat	...Pfannkuchen mit Schokolade
I don't like...	je n'aime pas...	Ich mag nicht...

...pancakes with lemon	...les crêpes au citron	...Pfannkuchen mit Zitrone
with sugar	au sucre	mit Zucker
with strawberry jam	à la confiture de fraises	mit Erdbeer- marmelade

English
I would like a pancake, please.
How much is a pancake?
Thank you. Goodbye!

French
Je voudrais une crêpe, s'il vous plaît.
C'est combien une crêpe ?
Merci. Au revoir !

German
Ich möchte einen Pfannkuchen, bitte.
Was kostet ein Pfannkuchen?
Danke. Auf Wiedersehen!

Animals in the Jungle assembly

Animals are a popular theme to study in primary schools and form the subject of a large number of familiar stories, from traditional tales to more modern classics. Well-known stories such as *Dear Zoo* by Rod Campbell (1982) and *Brown Bear, Brown Bear, What do I see...* by Martin and Carle (1967) are available in many languages and are easily adaptable for inspiring an assembly.

Create simple paper masks for the class to wear to make distinct groups of animals, or simply ask the children to wear a colour which represents an animal from the chosen story. Practise an action which represents the movement of the animal and a particular sound which they can perform in unison. Choose a small group of children to speak together to narrate the story or ask the questions, while the animals in turn respond. Keep the amount of language spoken by the animal groups to the minimum so that they respond confidently and with an action to reinforce their identity.

In this way you can proceed through the basic narrative of the story using the language given in the text. For *Dear Zoo* this would be the Narrators introducing each new animal sent by the zoo, the Animals saying why it was unsuitable, a Zoo Keeper saying *Oh dear!* or *Oh no!* and then *That's better!* at the end. For the *Brown Bear* book this would be the Narrators or the majority of the class asking what the animal could see and the groups of animals replying. At the end of the story, the animal groups could come forward and demonstrate what they could say and do: *I am a monkey and I'm called... I like bananas and I don't like apples. I live in the forest. I am eight years old.* All the animals together could perform an action rhyme showing movements and parts of their bodies, such as *this is my hand, this is my foot, I'm dancing, I'm climbing* etc. The finale could contain a song to the tune of *The Farmer's in His Den* as the whole class sing the equivalent of *The monkeys in the trees, The elephants in the water* etc. and *Oh yes, oh yes!* as a chorus.

English	French	German
Oh dear!	Oh la la !	Ach, je!
That's better	Ça va mieux	Das ist besser
I am a monkey...	Je suis un singe...	Ich bin ein Affe...
and I'm called...	...et je m'appelle	...und ich heiße...
I like apples	J'aime les pommes	Ich mag Äpfel
I don't like bananas	Je n'aime pas les bananes	Ich mag nicht Bananen
I live in the forest	J'habite dans la forêt	Ich lebe im Wald
I am eight years old	J'ai huit ans	Ich bin acht Jahre alt

This is my hand/my foot	Voici ma main, mon pied	Das ist mein Hand/mein Fuß
I'm dancing/climbing	Je danse/je grimpe	Ich tanze/klettere
The monkeys in the trees	Les singes dans les arbres	Die Affen in den Bäumen
The elephants in the water	Les éléphants dans l'eau	Die Elefanten im Wasser

Themed days
The European Day of Languages each September is a golden opportunity to celebrate the diversity of languages spoken in Europe and is also a great chance to spread the word about languages in your wider school community. Nine ideas which have proved very popular follow. Many more are available online (for example: www.bbc.co.uk/languages/edl/) as well as in Part Three, Project Three of *Living Languages: An Integrated Approach to Teaching Foreign Languages in Primary Schools* by Watts, Forder and Phillips (2013).

1 Invite native speakers who might be parents or helpers to read a short story or teach a simple song to a class.
2 Set up a whole school or year group quiz about the derivation of common words – can you guess which language they come from?
3 Set a homework task for all the school. How many words in different languages can you find to say *hello*?
4 Write to the parallel class in the new language in a partner school and invite them to an afternoon of parachute games (in the target language) in the school hall.
5 Invite a specialist teacher from the local secondary school to teach a few words of a totally new language. They might bring past pupils to show off their new skills and inspire younger children to have a go.
6 Set up one language activity per year group and swap them over throughout the day. They could be: food based, for example making pizza; geographical, for example matching capital

cities, monuments, rivers or currencies to a country in a quiz; arty, for example look at Matisse cut-out pictures and make some of your own; musical, for example listen to authentic lively music from the country and make up a dance etc.

7 Investigate links between the major European languages. Look at greetings words or numbers, *thank you, goodbye*. What similarities and differences can you spot?

8 If you are feeling bold and have a little rusty Latin, explore some common Latin words which have a familiar look, such as: *mater – mother; pater – father; miles – soldier*. Help the children to expand their vocabulary and see the links with English and other European languages. You'll be surprised how fascinated they can be.

9 Set up a poster competition across the school with an appropriate language theme: *thank you* in lots of languages; the name a country gives itself, for example *España*; landmarks and monuments from the major capital cities etc.

You certainly don't need to look very far to find a themed day. Above all, it is important to have fun celebrating!

CHAPTER 9
Starting to Write

The main focus for your early work in language learning will be developing oracy skills, encouraging children to listen, respond and communicate with each other. Over time, as children increase their understanding of the language, they will be introduced to a range of written forms of texts to extend their reading skills and at that stage they could begin to experiment with different forms of writing. Writing in the target language is a gradual process which needs to be built up slowly.

This chapter explores ways in which children can use a few words effectively to communicate with other people. It presents some straightforward examples of a range of writing activities which will encourage your class to develop this important skill, starting with the most simple, such as making lists, and gradually working towards the more complex involving writing simple stories in the target language.

LABELS AND CAPTIONS

One of the earliest writing tasks you set your class is likely to be copying from a selection of written words to write labels for display or captions for pictures and posters in the classroom. This might seem far too easy for children who can write in English already, but it is a stage that should not be missed and requires linking the written and spoken word and encourages concentration and careful checking of details.

Cross-curricular links
You could make a cross-curricular link in this way; for example, by attaching language labels of parts of the body to an existing

science display of bones in the skeleton or text to a display of weather conditions. Alternatively, this could be simply a language exercise with a self-drawn picture of a smiling face complete with speech bubble saying *Hello* in the target language and a series of labels for parts of the face.

Classroom equipment
Invite the class to write labels for classroom furniture, fixtures such as windows, sink etc. and any equipment; they can make a poster showing pens, rulers and pencil cases so that they can ask each other to pass them using the new language. This is a good opportunity to introduce a bilingual dictionary, which will be handy here for looking up unusual vocabulary.

Word banks
Make up some open-ended word banks on the wall which children can keep adding to with sticky labels, such as animal names, clothes names, verbs saying *I eat/ I walk*, memo words such as *See you soon, Cheerio*.

Grammatical word banks
Collect and organise words according to their function such as nouns and adverbs so that you reinforce a grammatical point as you stick up each new written word.

Instructions
Children write up any instructions which they hear you use in the classroom, for example *sit down, follow me* (see also Appendix 2 for some useful classroom language). Challenge the class to work out the negatives, for example, *don't sit down...* and add these next to each one.

Accent fun
Words in a new language often have accents or strange squiggly marks on letters. Turn this into an advantage by building up a bank every time you see a word with one of these marks. Set children challenges, for example group the words according to the kind of mark, investigate which letters are affected and work out how the sound is changed.

Collections

Make up weekly collections of a favourite kind of word, for example numbers/sports/ice creams/pets, or just a word your class has learned recently. Each person can write their favourite on a sticky label to add to the sheet. You could extend this to making a poster of everyone's birthday or favourite colour.

Super duper words

This could be your very exclusive group of the most fascinating new language words which the class encounter. Have a vote each week and a lucky person writes this up to add to a growing collection.

MAKING LISTS

Another popular way to introduce writing in short bursts is to ask children to make quick lists. Make sure that you relate the list to vocabulary which you have just taught and have the relevant flashcards and text in front of the class. The children could use mini-whiteboards and pens or just paper and pencils. Try to make it fun by giving them a time limit, for example, you could say: *In three minutes write a list of your five favourite foods.* Although this might seem at first glance far too easy, the children do have to read, understand and make a choice before writing their chosen words carefully and accurately. Try to rotate who reads out their list at the end or ask everyone to read out their favourite example. Children love this activity as they can all contribute something and feel that they have made a big step choosing their own favourites.

Groups of five

For beginners, start with five colours, five numbers, five parts of the face etc. More advanced groups still benefit from this activity and could try five picnic foods, five things to do at the weekend, five things you do every morning, for example: *I clean my teeth, I have my breakfast.* Other lists could include as many months as possible in two minutes, the days of the week as fast as you can, three animals you might find in the zoo/in the jungle/on the farm.

To extend these challenges, ask children to add an adjective, for example a small nose/tall lion etc. or add a colour to the noun (checking that the position of the adjective and its agreement with the noun is correct).

DESIGNING MENUS

Another way of selecting and copying favourite words is to ask children to devise sections of a menu under headings which you provide. If you have been working on breakfasts, both food and drink, each table could work on a different course of a meal, writing the different options available. These could be in temporary sticky-label form or written out more formally and illustrated for a class book in the book corner. Alternatively, children could decide on the name of their own café or restaurant and set out their different courses.

Horrible food
Conjure up some revolting or bizarre choices for food or drinks, using unappetising colours or flavours, for example green croissants, blue bananas, orange milk. More experienced children could make up a magic potion or brew for a spell.

English	French	German
menu	le menu du jour	die Speisekarte
first course/starters	les hors-d'œuvres	die Vorspeise
main course	le plat principal	das Hauptgericht
desserts	les desserts	der Nachtisch
drinks	les boissons	die Getränke
breakfast	le petit déjeuner	das Frühstück

In particular, children love to design menus for different kinds of food outlets. Look for opportunities for them to add details to a basic foodstuff. Popular examples could be making up posters for a pizza shop, a crêperie, a sandwich shop, an ice cream kiosk etc., where you can start with the standard food, such as a sandwich, and then be inventive with the fillings. Alternatively you could opt for a baguette shop, a series of fruit tarts in a bakery or a milk shake parlour. There's a recipe in Chapter 5, 'Being Creative', for a milk shake you can all make together.

English	French	German
sandwich	le sandwich	das Sandwich
ice cream	la glace	das Eis
pizza	la pizza	die Pizza
pancake	la crêpe	der Pfannkuchen
baguette	la baguette	das belegte Brot
tart	la tarte	der Obstkuchen
with cheese	au fromage	mit Käse
with ham	au jambon	mit Schinken
with tuna	au thon	mit Thunfisch
with mushrooms	aux champignons	mit Pilzen
with chocolate	au chocolat	mit Schokolade
with strawberries	à la fraise	mit Erdbeeren
with bananas	à la banane	mit Bananen
with vanilla	à la vanille	mit Vanille
with lemon	au citron	mit Zitrone

FAVOURITE LIKES AND DISLIKES

A simple starting point for expressing an opinion is for children to write what they like, don't like, love or hate. This is a versatile idea which can be used with many topics: animals; food; drinks; lessons; hobbies etc. Start by just asking your class to write a short statement about something they like and something they don't like. The sentences could be contained in suitably shaped pictures such as a heart and a heart with a line through the middle.

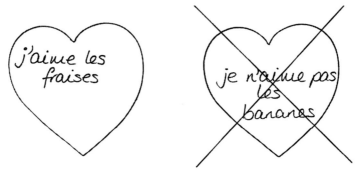

Figure 9.1 Likes and Dislikes

As a second stage, teach your class the connectives for *and* and *but*. This enables the children to extend the sentence and form something like this (in the context here of fruit):

English
I like strawberries **but** I don't like bananas.

French
J'aime les fraises **mais** je n'aime pas les bananes.

German
Ich mag Erdbeeren **aber** ich mag nicht Bananen.

MY SHOPPING

A good activity based on shopping is to create shopping lists using the essential verb structure *I would like...* and suitable polite phrases to smooth the way. Children could write a series of ice-cream orders or vegetable and fruit items. In addition, don't forget to introduce the class to quantities of food. How many times have adults been stuck in a foreign supermarket trying to conjure up the words for half a kilo or 100 grams? Teach them early and they can prompt their parents or, better still, do the shopping for them!

English	French	German
I would like...	Je voudrais...	Ich möchte...
please	s'il vous plaît	bitte
thank you!	merci !	Dankeschön!
a kilo/ half a kilo	un kilo/ un demi-kilo	ein Kilo/ ein halbes Kilo
100 grams	100 grammes	100 Gramm
a packet of...	un paquet de...	ein Paket...
a bottle of...	une bouteille de...	eine Flasche...
a tin of...	une boîte de...	eine Dose...

WHO AM I?

Guessing games intrigue children, especially when they are based on themselves. Ask children to write a few facts about themselves on subjects which they have already covered such as their age, how many brothers/sisters they have, their hair/eye colour. They could write these statements in a speech bubble or on the back of a photograph or hand drawn picture of themselves so that class-mates can guess the answer and check on the reverse. This also works well when applied to an animal picture where children provide clues on the reverse.

SPEECH BUBBLES

Write speech bubbles with or without an attached face to greet visitors to the classroom giving a *hello, welcome, my name is..., I am aged....* More experienced classes could add details of favourite school subjects, birthday dates, hobbies.

MINI-DIARY

Use your poster of days of the week to spur you on to a short sequence about what you do during the week. Start with the name of each day and add a different statement each time describing something you eat, do etc. This could fit into a daily classroom routine where children make up their diary sentence just before they go home or just after lunch. More advanced classes could add a time to the mixture, for example: *On Monday at eight o'clock I eat a croissant.*

MORE COMPLEX WRITING: SIMILE DESCRIPTIONS

Children learn how to recognise and write their own similes throughout literacy lessons in primary school and it is easy to adapt them to a new language. Children enjoy the fun of strange comparisons and can be very creative in their pairings of words. It helps if you steer them towards a collection of nouns to use, such as animal names, and this can be a good first step for consulting a dual-language dictionary.

Steps:

1 First, look at some easy examples in English to refresh memories, for example: *as busy as a bee; as big as a bus.*
2 Children build their own animal word list using a dual-language dictionary. They will need a minimum of ten words to choose from. Lists of farm and rainforest animals in the target language can be found in Chapter 5, 'Being Creative', as can a list of sea creatures. Children should make sure that they note

the gender of each noun so that they can add the appropriate article later (for example, a tiger in French is *un tigre*. In German it is *der Tiger*).

3 Now choose some appropriate adjectives to describe the characteristics of the animals. As far as possible, use adjectives which the class have already come across and which will be useful in the future rather than searching for obscure words from the dictionary which will not be used again. Useful ones could include the following:

English	French	German
small	petit(e)	klein
large	grand(e)	groß
happy	heureux/heureuse	glücklich
unhappy	malheureux/ malheureuse	unglücklich
kind	gentil/gentille	freundlich
shy	timide	schüchtern
fierce	féroce	wild
angry	fâché(e)	wütend
enormous	énorme	enorm
sad	triste	traurig
tired	fatigué(e)	müde
naughty	méchant(e)	ungezogen

4 Put the two groups of words together with a word between them meaning *like* (in French *comme*; in German *wie*). So you have *grand comme un tigre* in French and *groß wie ein Tiger* in German, for *as big as a tiger*. You could leave this exercise here and ask children to write out a brilliant collection of similes for a display, to be put up alongside pictures of named animals.

Extension Activities:

1 Make silly similes by connecting unlikely pairs such as *fierce like a rabbit.*
2 Children draw a circle with a small picture of an animal inside and create a spider-gram of similes around, comparing it to other animals.
3 If you want to extend the language used, teach the words for *I am* and place them at the start of the sentence so that you can do a series of similes about yourself. So in French you will have *Je suis grand comme un tigre* or in German *Ich bin groß wie ein Tiger.* As an alternative, children could write similes for their friends or family.
4 You could add another layer to the similes by creating your weekly diary of similes about yourself. Just add a day of the week at the start of each sentence and suggest that you feel like a different animal each day. For example: *On Monday I am shy like a mouse, on Tuesday I am fierce like a lion* etc. In French this will be *lundi je suis timide comme une souris*, whilst in German you will have *Dienstag bin ich wild wie ein Tiger* for example. Note the position of the verb in German if you do not start with the subject.

COMMUNICATING

Writing cards

Everyone seems to like receiving a card and the children in your class will be no exception! Ask them to design a card each (perhaps as part of an art class) and then write an appropriate message inside in the target language. Here is a list of suitable occasions and the words you could put inside the cards:

English	French	German
Happy Christmas	Joyeux Noël	Frohe Weihnachten
Happy Easter	Joyeuses Pâques	Frohe Ostern
Get well soon	Remets-toi vite	Gute Besserung
Good luck	Bonne chance	Viel Glück
I love you	Je t'aime	Ich liebe dich
Happy Birthday	Joyeux anniversaire	herzlichen Glückwunsch zum Geburtstag

Some lovely pop-up cards are presented in Chapter Two (Project Six) of *Living Languages: An Integrated Approach to Teaching Foreign Languages in Primary Schools* (Watts, Forder and Phillips, 2013) which you could make with your class. Or you could send an e-card. This website has some good ideas in German: www.helles-koepfchen.de/e-cards/.

Writing and sending e-mails
Sending an e-mail to a person or group of people in the target language is very exciting to many children – especially when the reply comes back as it usually does on the same day! Using e-mail in your language classes certainly extends what you can do in the classroom, as it locates the target language firmly in the real world of everyday electronic communication. All you need to get going is a class of enthusiastic learners, a reasonable computer with relevant software and someone to communicate with in the target language. Regarding the latter, a relevant website is *British Council Schools Online* (previously known as *Global Gateway*) which works in many countries offering school partnerships among other things. See schoolsonline.britishcouncil.org/partner-with-a-school for further details.

Sending e-mails with your class provides an invaluable context for communicating with other speakers in authentic situations. They offer your children practice in reading and writing as well as speaking and discussion around what to say and what the reply might mean. You can link the content of the e-mail to topics covered in class and send photographs of the work produced as well. For example, if your topic is 'Healthy Eating', your children can describe what they have in their lunch boxes and send photographs of the same to their partner school. Or they could send a photo of the school vegetable patch with seedlings labelled in the target language. The replies may or may not revolve around a similar topic, depending on whether or not lunch boxes are a feature of the day, but they are bound to offer some culturally specific and interesting alternatives!

Here is a possible way to start with your first class e-mail to a partner school. The language needs to be as simple as possible and the sentences kept short in the first instance.

English
Dear X. We are class X. Our school is in (town). We are learning (French/German). How are you? Best wishes, X.

French
Cher/Chère X. Nous sommes la classe X. Notre école est à (ville). Nous apprenons le français. Comment allez-vous ? Meilleurs vœux, X.

German
Liebe(r) X. Wir sind Klasse X. Unsere Schule ist in (Stadt). Wir lernen Deutsch. Wie geht's? Beste Wünsche, X.

Writing a postcard
Postcards have a certain novelty value in this age of electronic communication and many children like to receive one as much as they like sending them! The stamps from other countries are often very interesting and make a good discussion point in your class, as can the picture on the front of the card. A simple postcard in German can be found on the UK–German Connection's website, which makes a good starting point (see: www.ukgermanconnection.org/kids-send-postcard). The only thing you need is someone to send the postcard to (see above for ways to involve a partner school). The

actual substance of your postcard can be built up over time. Why not start out with a simple statement followed by a question to which the partner can respond. Here is an example:

English
Dear X,
Today it is snowing! Snow is fun! What is your weather like?
Love from X

French
Cher/Chère X,
Aujourd'hui il neige ! La neige est amusant. Quel temps fait-il chez toi ?
Amicalement, X

German
Liebe(r) X
Heute schneit es! Schnee macht Spaß! Wie ist dein Wetter?
Gruß von X

Here are some other weather expressions you could use:

English	French	German
It's sunny	Il y a du soleil	Es ist sonnig
It's hot	Il fait chaud	Es ist heiß
It's raining	Il pleut	Es regnet
It's cold	Il fait froid	Es ist kalt
It's windy	Il y a du vent	Es ist windig

An inspirational book by Emily Gravett (2007) called *Meerkat Mail* tells the story of a meerkat who travels the world and sends postcards back to his family from different places. However, on many of the postcards there is a problem, often because the meerkat does not like the habitat where he is (it is too hot, too cold etc.). You could easily adapt this idea in your language classes by choosing an animal and following his or her travels around the world (an excellent way of incorporating cultural information as well) and sending postcards back to folk at home.

SIMPLE POEMS

Writing a poem in a foreign language can seem a little daunting at first. However, it is good fun and an excellent way to consolidate language towards the end of a topic, as well as offering an effective way of focusing on pronunciation. Poetry writing involves the whole class, as suggestions can be made by everyone. Remember that a little language goes a long way, as long as the children recognise that the poems do not have to be very long, do not have to rhyme and do not have to include whole sentences! Poems produced within this framework have the appealing freshness of early poetry writing and mirror work done in literacy classes, where the emphasis is on creativity and imagination.

Tips: keep the writing in the present tense to make it easier. Start with a whole class poem before asking the children to write their own versions.

Quick poem
A poem can be created quickly by addressing the following questions.

English	French	German
What am I?	Que suis-je ?	Was bin ich?
What colour am I?	Quelle couleur suis-je ?	Welche Farbe bin ich?
What size?	Quelle taille suis-je ?	Wie groß bin ich?
Where do I live?	J'habite où ?	Wo lebe ich?
What do I eat?	Qu'est-ce que je mange ?	Was fresse ich?

Your poem then is formed from the answers to these questions.

English	French	German
I am a butterfly.	Je suis un papillon.	Ich bin ein Schmetterling.
I am colourful.	Je suis coloré.	Ich bin bunt.
I am small.	Je suis petit.	Ich bin klein.
I live in the flowers.	J'habite dans les fleurs.	Ich lebe in den Blumen.
I eat insects.	Je mange des insectes.	Ich fresse Insekten.

Figure 9.2 A Butterfly to Decorate

So your class poem will be something along these lines:

French
Un papillon. Coloré, petit. Habite dans les fleurs. Mange des insectes. Bon appétit Monsieur Papillon !

German
Ein Schmetterling. Bunt, klein. Lebt in den Blumen. Frißt Insekten. Guten Appetit Herr Schmetterling!

Your class can decorate their butterflies and hang them around the classroom with their poems.

IN THE MAGIC MIRROR

(French: Dans le miroir magique; German: Im Zauberspiegel)
This title invites the writer to suggest mismatching images, unusual juxtapositions of nouns and verbs. You could take a whimsical and rather frivolous theme to get the class started on the idea of writing in another language using their imagination and natural creativity.

Resources: a class set of bilingual dictionaries.

Tip: you can make beautiful, framed mirrors using baking foil for the glass, to display the classwork at the end of the day.

Steps:

1 Decide on your category of nouns. They could be: family members; professions, such as a doctor; animals; a type of creature – for example, a bird poem about different kinds of bird. Once the category is decided, the children will need a bilingual dictionary to make their own glossary of about a dozen possible nouns and meanings.
2 The next step is to collect in the same way a selection of interesting verbs which will contrast with the nouns. They could be verbs describing movement, sound etc., or even the daily

routine verbs which everyone encounters describing how they get up in the morning. Keep all the verbs in the third person singular to agree with s/he (in French *il* or *elle* and in German *er* or *sie*). Watch out for common irregular verbs. Normally a dictionary has a section for these so do check first.

3 You may also need some adverbs to make your sentences more interesting and to add to the action.

4 A key teaching element will be to introduce the word *who* (French: *qui*; German *der, die* or *das*) to connect the two parts of the sentence. **Note**: in German the verb in the second clause, after the word for *who*, needs to go to the end. In German it is easier to start the sentence with the subject as well (see examples below).

Ma famille

If you opt for family members, try to create a wistful combination of phrases, suggesting what they might be doing if each were completely alone. Your framework is thus: *in the magic mirror I see* (family member) *who is* (verb) (adverb).

Family members can easily be researched in a dictionary to achieve sentences such as the three that follow:

(...I see my brother crying softly)

French: Dans le miroir magique je vois mon frère qui pleure doucement.

German: Ich sehe im Zauberspiegel meinen Bruder, der leise weint.

(...I see my aunt dancing slowly)

French: Dans le miroir magique je vois ma tante qui danse lentement.

German: Ich sehe im Zauberspiegel meine Tante, die langsam tanzt.

(...I see my father laughing madly)

French: Dans le miroir magique je vois mon père qui rit fortement.

German: Ich sehe im Zauberspiegel meinen Vater, der verrückt lacht.

There are variations of the Magic Mirror poem in Chapter Six (Project Seven) of *Living Languages: An Integrated Approach to Teaching Foreign Languages in Primary Schools* (Watts, Forder and Phillips, 2013). Topics include: birds; in the enchanted garden; in the treasure chest; myself; the New Year; in the dark wood).

SIMPLE STORIES

Creating an imaginative, simple book
Making a simple book with your class is an inspiring way to use language creatively. The little book described here is an ideal way to provide opportunities for communication in a language, or a class display, or to keep on the class bookshelves for story time. Your children could take the book home too to tell stories with their families and teach them the little conversations.

Resources: card; scissors; binding for class book, for example spiral binder or treasury tags.

Tip: make sure you try out the ideas in advance and have a template ready to show the class what the end product should resemble.

Writing a half-and-half book
This example consists of a page contributed by each student divided into an upper and lower half. When each page is complete, a whole book can be put together and the pages cut across the middle to make a mismatching book. The example given is about an animal and its habitat, but could easily be adapted to many other topics.

Steps:

1 Each child has a piece of A4 card of any colour.
2 Lightly draw a line half way down the page **across** the page to divide the page into two sections.
3 In the top half, ask the children to draw an animal to fill up the space, colour it in a lively way and label it in the target language to say, for example, *an elephant lives...* (**French:** *un éléphant habite...*; **German:** *ein Elefant lebt...*).
4 In the bottom half, draw the habitat of the animal, colour it and label it in the target language, for example *in the jungle* (**French:** *dans la jungle*; **German:** *im Dschungel*).
5 Encourage the children to draw different animals from each other; even birds or fish, as long as they know the target language for them (a small class dictionary might help here and you will need some suggestions up your sleeve too!). Try to get thirty different species from the class. Similarly, try to accumulate different habitats. Lists of useful vocabulary for animals, both on the farm and in the rainforest, are presented in Chapter 5, 'Being Creative'.

English	French	German
in the desert	dans le désert	in der Wüste
on the farm	à la ferme	auf dem Bauernhof
in the air	dans l'air	in der Luft
in the sea	dans la mer	im Meer
in the forest	dans la forêt	im Wald
at home	dans la maison	zu Hause
in the zoo	au zoo	im Zoo
in a tree	dans un arbre	in einem Baum
underground	sous la terre	unter der Erde
in a nest	dans un nid	in einem Nest

6 Gather together all the finished card pages and assemble in a mixed order so that you have a jumble of different animals rather than all the fish together.

7 Make a front cover, for example *Where do you live?* (**French:** *Où habites-tu* ? **German:** *Wo lebst du?*) and include a good animal picture too from a child. You may also want to add a strong piece of plain card at the end to keep the book firmly in place.

8 If you have access to a spiral binder, use it to put the book together. If not, make four holes down the left side of the pages with a strong hole punch and attach all the pages and covers with treasury tags.

9 With a strong pair of scissors, carefully cut along the midway lines of each page, **but not the front and back covers**, to separate each page into its two halves.

10 You should now have a half-and-half funny book of matches and mismatches of animals and their habitats.

11 Open the book at any animal and then turn the lower sections to find a 'wrong' habitat.

12 Choose a couple of children to find random animals and habitats every day and read them aloud.

Alternatives

Try other themes for a half-and-half book. Here are some suggestions: an animal word and its food, for example *a rabbit eats carrots*; rooms of the house and something you would do there, for example *in the kitchen I eat my breakfast*; something to eat which goes with something else to eat, for example *fish and chips*; going somewhere by a particular means of transport, for example *going to school by bus*.

Mini pocket-book

Children enjoy making little books to fit a short piece of writing. There are a variety of different kinds which are simple for small hands to execute. One example is a fold-up mini-book with a pocket for a character to be placed in and taken on a journey. This format suits the story of a character on a journey, travelling from one country to another or moving from place to place around a local area or around a building.

The example given is loosely based on cross-curricular work on the familiar geography topic of Katie Morag and her home in the Scottish Islands (Hedderwick, 1985). A little story could describe the places where she might travel around her island, or any character might go on an imaginary island.

Alternative themes could be:

* a trip around a zoo to see a variety of animals;
* a walk to different locations in your school;
* a shopping trip along the high street going into several shops;
* a visit to the seaside looking at a range of attractions;
* a round trip to European capitals, looking at their main tourist sites.

First, using a bilingual dictionary, make a list of places which might be visited. For an island story, the setting could be: the beach (**French:** *la plage;* **German:** *der Strand*) the post office (**French:** *le bureau de poste;* **German:** *das Postamt*); the farm (**French:** *la ferme;* **German:** *der Bauernhof*); the hill (**French:** *la colline;* **German:** *der Hügel*); the loch/lake (**French:** *le lac;* **German:** *der See*); the school (**French:** *l'école;* **German:** *die Schule*); the house (**French:** *la maison;* **German:** *das Haus*).

Steps:

1 Begin with the title: where is Katie/Matthew? (**French:** *Où est Katie/Matthew?* **German:** *Wo ist Katie/Matthew?*).
2 Start the story with *Katie goes...* (**French:** *Katie va...;* **German:** *Katie geht...*) and add the destinations using in French *au, à la, à l'* and in German *zum, zur* according to the gender of the destination.

In **French** this text would read: *Katie va à la colline, elle va à la ferme, elle va à l'école, elle va à la maison, elle va à la plage, elle va au bureau de poste, elle va au lac.*

In **German** the text would be: *Katie geht zum Strand, sie geht zum Postamt, sie geht zum Bauernhof, sie geht zum Hügel, sie geht zum See. Sie geht zur Schule, sie geht zum Haus.*

Steps:

1 To make the book, take a piece of A4 paper or card. Fold it in half lengthways and keep the fold at the top.
2 Fold it in half across the width of the page and place the new fold to the left like the spine of a book.
3 Take the further edge of the front page (on your right) and fold it back to join the left hand spine. Press down the new fold half way along the width of the book.
4 Turn the book over onto the back and do the same: fold the furthest edge over to join the left hand spine and make a new fold.
5 To finish, make sure that your lengthways fold is at the top of your book and adjust your folding book so that it flows from front to back. You now have the possibility of eight pages or seven plus the title page. If this is too many, keep it to a four-page book just on the front pages of your book. Write your text on each page and illustrate appropriately.
6 As a final flourish, make a small square card to stick or staple to the title page to make a little pocket. Decorate it with a picture of a flower or tree or something in keeping with your journey. Draw onto a separate piece of card a picture of your main character dressed in suitable clothes, colour in brightly, laminate and cut out. Attach a piece of wool or string to the back of the figure with sticky tape and stick the other end inside the little pocket, out of sight.
7 Now take your character out for a walk to all the places in your story. Each person can make up their own story, visiting places in any order, or the teacher could recount the story in French or German while the class take their characters for a walk to the places mentioned in the correct order.

CHAPTER 10
At the End of the Day

This final chapter is all about the end of your lessons. It contains a range of short, simple and fun ways to wind down at the end of the school day, whilst revising structures learned in context. The focus here is on consolidation rather than the presentation of new language and this chapter offers children a quieter space for thinking about what they have already learned before they go home. It is designed around those few moments at the end of a busy day when everything has been tidied away and the only resources available are the teacher, the board, a few simple items and your classroom displays.

QUICK GAMES

Spot the Accent
Put up ten or so words with accents on some letters or any other mark used in the language. Children work out which ones have got exactly the same accent and when they are all matched up, everyone chants them in unison.

Make a Date/ Make a Time
Put on the board or wall a quick series of dates in the language, one after the other. They could just be days of the week or more complicated dates including months and numbers, depending on what has been taught.

Children call out together what the date is in English in quick response as fast as you put up each card or, when you show a clock time on a cardboard clock, they call it out in the target language.

Day Times
Put up flashcards with text to show the times of day such as morning, afternoon, evening and separately, days of the week. Challenge children to put together one from each section to make a time of day, for example *Monday morning*. Alternatively they could write on a mini-whiteboard as many day/time combinations as possible in one minute. Rapidly go round the room with everyone saying one. (In French it would be *lundi matin, mardi soir* etc. In German you would have *Montagmorgen, Dienstagabend* etc.).

English
morning, afternoon, evening, night

French
matin, après-midi, soir, nuit

German
Morgen, Nachmittag, Abend, Nacht

Alliterations
Going round the room, each person says their name and then adds the phrase *and I am a...* and names an animal beginning with the same letter as their own name, for example: *Je m'appelle Simon et je suis un singe; Ich heiße Kathy und ich bin ein Kaninchen.* Have a list of possible animals on the board to help and suggest that people choose their surname if there isn't an obvious match for their first name.

Animal Rap
Perform a simple animal rap either sitting down or on your feet making appropriate actions. Here's a simple one:

English	French	German
A lion runs	Un lion court	Ein Löwe läuft
A monkey climbs	Un singe grimpe	Ein Affe klettert
A crocodile swims	Un crocodile nage	Ein Krokodil schwimmt
As for me, I dance!	Mais moi, je danse !	Aber ich, ich tanze!

Packing Up

Put up a picture of a simple suitcase on the board or ask a child to draw one. Tell the class that you are going on holiday and they must choose what you take with you. Decide what the weather will be like and let them loose! The ideas can be sensible or ridiculous; it doesn't matter as long as they use the target language.

Doctor, Doctor

A volunteer comes to the front and winces with pain. Everyone calls out *Doctor, doctor*! Children have to guess which bit hurts (see Chapter 4, 'On Your Feet', for vocabulary).

French: Monsieur Médecin, Monsieur Médecin!

German: Herr Doktor, Herr Doktor!

Treasure Hunt

You could play this with just one bag of treasure for the whole class or with two bags if you want to have two competing teams. In advance, put five or six items which the children can name in the language in a bag such as a set of different coloured cards or a set of animals or food. A volunteer (or one each from both teams) comes up to the front and has to rummage in the bag to find the item you name with everyone else counting loudly up to ten. Make sure you do a countdown dramatically before saying the name of the item. You could make it more difficult by asking the

child to put on a funny hat and gloves first while everyone practises counting or anything else which adds to the fun.

Spot the Verb/Noun etc.
Put up six or so known words on the board, some of which are
nouns with their gender and some of which are verbs. Children
spot the verbs and explain how they worked it out. Play the same
game with other word classes and encourage children to define
what a verb/noun etc. is in English.

Odd One Out
This is a similar game to the one above, with just one word in a
different class to the others (i.e. five verbs and one adjective).
Don't give any clues about the word classes involved and ask
children to name them all, for example, noun, adjective, adverb.

Feminine or Masculine?
Put up a list of nouns with their articles (for example *le* and *la* in
French and *der, die* and *das* in German) and ask children which
are feminine and which are masculine (and, in the case of German,
which are neuter). Add some which begin with *un* or *une* (masculine and feminine for *a/ an* in French) and *ein, eine* and *ein*
(masculine, feminine and neuter for *a/ an* in German) and repeat
the process. Encourage children to make links. (In French, *le* is
used to say *the* and *un* is used to say *a/ an* for masculine nouns; *la*
and *une* for feminine nouns. In German masculine nouns are indicated by *der* for *the* and *ein* for *a/ an*, *die* and *eine* are the
equivalent for feminine nouns, whilst *das* indicates *the* for neuter
nouns and *ein* is used for *a/ an*.)

What's My Question?
Put up a jumbled mix of common questions and answers. Ask children to match them.

Where's the Puppet?
Put a box on a table in front of the class and hold a familiar puppet
or toy in front of it. Use the words for *behind/ in front/ next to* etc.
(see Chapter 4, 'On Your Feet', for vocabulary) and ask a volunteer
to put the puppet in the box in the way you describe. Next, you

put the puppet in the place and the children tell you the correct phrase to describe its position.

THE MEMORY TRAY

This is a favourite activity which is both simple to organise and fun to take part in. The teacher displays up to ten items (or pictures of the items) on a tray. The items should relate to language that students already know.

Resources: a tray with either real items or pictures of real items on it and a cloth large enough to cover the whole tray.

Example:

English	French	German
ruler	la règle	das Lineal
rubber	la gomme	der Radiergummi
pencil	le crayon	der Bleistift
pencil sharpener	le taille-crayon	der Spitzer
felt pen	le stylo-feutre	der Filzschreiber
calculator	la calculatrice	der Rechner
paper	le papier	das Papier
book	le livre	das Buch

Steps:

1 Allow the children enough time to look at the items and memorise them (about three minutes). You could label the items on the tray to help the children remember the words they need. If you do this, make sure the labels are large enough for everyone to read easily.
2 Cover the tray with a cloth and turn away from the class so that the children cannot see what you are doing.

3 Remove one item from the tray and hide it.
4 Turn back to the class and ask *What is missing?*
5 Children have one minute to look quickly at the remaining items on the tray and identify which one is missing. They must name the missing object in the target language using the correct gender.

HANGMAN

This is a traditional word game which is a useful way to end the school day. The important thing about it is to agree beforehand with your class what the hanged person will look like. You do not want any arguments at the end of the game about whether or not the hanged person should have a nose or strands of hair! The simplest end result is as follows:

Figure 10.1 Hangman

Steps:

1 Draw the hanged person you will end up with in one small corner of the board to prevent any further discussion!

2 Choose a word from your lesson or recent topic and draw space markers for each letter in the word. The word *Bruder* in German (*brother*) would be represented thus: _ _ _ _ _ _.

3 Children take it in turns to guess a missing letter using the target language if possible (alphabets in German and French are included in Appendix 1).

4 If the letter is correct, add it to the space marker(s). If the letter is incorrect, you can add it to a list in one corner of the board and draw one line of your hanged person.

5 If a child thinks s/he knows what the word is, s/he can make a guess. An incorrect guess means you draw another line on your hanged person. The aim of the game is for the children to guess the word before the picture of the hanged person is completed. Once this has been done, ask a child to come out and choose a word (they should check the spelling with you first and it is easier for the child if the letters are called out in the mother tongue).

TRAFFIC LIGHTS

This lively, moving-around game is good fun and ends quietly with the children lying still on the floor having all suffered a puncture!

Resources: you will need a transport frieze running around the classroom wall(s) with different vehicles labelled in the target language(s) (see 'Make a Wall Frieze' in Chapter 5, 'Being Creative').

Steps:

1 Ask each child to look at the wall frieze and select their favourite vehicle in their mind.

2 Then ask each child which one s/he is, by using this simple exchange:

Teacher: *Qu'est ce-que tu es ? Was bist du? What are you?*
Child: *Je suis un vélo/ une voiture* etc.; *Ich bin ein Fahrrad/ ein Auto* etc.; *I am a bicycle/ a car* etc.

3 Remind the class of the colours which you will use in the game: red; green; orange; black (**French:** *rouge; vert; orange; noir;* **German:** *rot; grün; orange; schwarz*).

4 Tell the children to listen out carefully for the colour you call. The colours represent these actions: red = stop (children stand still); green = go (children walk around the classroom); orange = prepare to go (children get into a start position); black = puncture (children fall down and lie still on the floor).

5 On green, the children set off 'driving' their chosen vehicle. They follow your instructions using the colours until you call out *black*, whereupon everyone falls down and lies quietly on the floor.

WEATHER MIME GAME

Miming words and phrases always goes down well at the end of the day and is also an effective way for you to make sure that the children have understood key vocabulary. The game is simple: you say a word and the children perform a mime to represent the word you give. The mime can be one you have worked out with your class as part of the normal classroom routine, or it could be one that the children make up on the spur of the moment. Any topic can trigger a good range of mimes. The example below focuses on the weather.

English	French	German	mime
It's hot	Il fait chaud	Es ist heiß	Children mop brows
It's cold	Il fait froid	Es ist kalt	Children shiver
It's raining	Il pleut	Es regnet	Children make raindrops falling with fingers
It's snowing	Il neige	Es schneit	Children throw snowballs at each other
It's windy	Il y a du vent	Es ist windig	Children puff and blow!
It's stormy	Il y a de l'orage	Es ist stürmisch	Children cut lightning patterns in the air with hands

SIMON SAYS...

This is another classroom favourite, which involves everyone listening carefully to your instructions. The French version is called *Jacques a dit*, whilst in German it can be known as *Simon sagt*. You give the class a series of simple commands. If the commands start with either *Jacques a dit*, or *Simon sagt* the children and you should carry out the command. However, if the command does not start with the phrase, then the children should stay still even if you make the move yourself to try to catch them out! The winner is the last child (or small group) standing!

French

Jacques a dit: 'Asseyez vous !'	(Simon says: 'Sit down!')
Jacques a dit: 'Touchez la tête !'	(Simon says: 'Touch your head!')
Jacques a dit: 'Touchez le nez !'	(Simon says: 'Touch your nose!')
'Levez les mains !'	('Put your hands in the air!')

German

Simon sagt: 'Setzt euch!'	(Simon says: 'Sit down!')
Simon sagt: 'Zeigt auf den Kopf!'	(Simon says: 'Touch your head!')
Simon sagt: 'Zeigt auf die Nase!'	(Simon says: 'Touch your nose!')
'Hände hoch!'	('Put your hands in the air!')

ANIMAL CHARADES

One child comes to the front of the class and thinks of an animal. S/he points to anyone in the class and whispers the name of the animal in the target language. The child indicated acts out the animal. For example, an elephant would swing its trunk, a monkey would scratch its armpits perhaps, a snake would slither about and a cat might wash its whiskers. If the other children can guess what the animal is and it is correct, the child who has just acted the animal changes places with the child at the front and so the game continues.

TONGUE TWISTERS

Tongue twisters seem to have an endless fascination, especially for primary-aged children, and there is even an *International Tongue Twister Day* on November 7th each year. But you don't have to save your tongue twisters for that date only! They are a great way to practise pronunciation and just to play around with the target language, especially at the end of the day when everyone is sitting quietly. You need to have the words on display somewhere so that everyone can see them – why not try some of the examples below and see how quickly your class can say them without tripping over their tongues! It is also great fun and relatively simple to write your own to practise new words you have recently taught in your language classes. You could try doing this together with your class as well!

French
Sept serpents sont sur la chaise.
(*Seven snakes are on the chair.*)
Un chasseur en chemise à cheval.
(*A hunter in a shirt on horseback.*)
Trois tortues trottent sur un trottoir très étroit.
(*Three turtles trot along a very narrow pavement.*)

German
Ein schwarzes Schwein hat einen schwarzen Schwanz.
(*A black pig has a black tail.*)
Sechs Schlangen schlängeln sich im Schloβ.
(*Six snakes wriggle in the castle.*)
Kluge Katzen kratzen keine Krokodile.
(*Clever cats don't scratch crocodiles.*)

FINGER RHYMES

There are lots of little rhymes which the children can learn and demonstrate using only their fingers. www.mamalisa.com for example has a lovely selection of little rhymes, songs and other verses, as does www.german.about.com and www.french.about.com. In the one that follows in German, the children point to the body parts as they are mentioned following your model and then fall down on the floor at the end.

Die Schneeflocke	**The snowflake**
Sanft und ruhig die	Softly and quietly
Schneeflocke fällt nach	the snowflake falls
unten.	downwards.
Sie tropft von den	It drops from your
Augen auf die Nase,	eyes to your nose,
Von der Nase auf den	From your nose to
Mund.	your mouth.
Immer nach unten –	Always downwards –
am Kinn vorbei	past your chin
Bis auf den Bauch wo	Until your stomach
sie sich ausruht.	where it rests awhile.
Dann tropft sie leise	Then it drops quietly
auf die Erde	to the ground
Und ist nicht mehr zu sehen!	And disappears!

The following little rhyme in French can be learnt by heart. Try chanting the rhyme in different voices, for example,you could chant the days of the week softly at first, getting louder as the week progresses, and the final word *Sunday* can end with a shout! Or half the class could say the numbers aloud using their fingers to count them off and the other half could name the days of the week in the target language.

Il y a sept jours dans une semaine/ There are seven days in a week		
un	lundi	Monday
deux	mardi	Tuesday
trois	mercredi	Wednesday
quatre	jeudi	Thursday
cinq	vendredi	Friday
six	samedi	Saturday
sept	dimanche	Sunday

MYSTERY OBJECT

This popular game involves looking at the world from an unusual angle and guessing what the object is.

Resources: you will need a selection of photographs of objects that the children know and can label in the target language, but which show only part of the whole object. You could build up this bank yourself by cropping photographs which you have taken or asking your class to help you. Once your collection is complete, you could make it last longer by laminating the pictures and sharing it with other classes in your school.

- The photographs could be used as a slide show and quiz on the interactive whiteboard, with the children guessing the object. Alternatively, the laminated version could be used by the children at their tables. However, at the end of the school day the interactive whiteboard is more useful perhaps, as there will be less to tidy up and the children may well be sitting on the floor.
- When choosing objects to photograph, think about your topics covered in class and what is practicable to photograph. Photographs of wild animals are distinctly harder to photograph than members of your family wearing different items of clothing, for example!
- You can return to the photographs periodically, as repeated activities are often very popular. Your photographs could also go on the display table for a while and the children could ask the adults around them to guess what they are – using the target language of course!

THE BOX OF SURPRISES

This is a simple guessing game where you give the clues to the class and the children guess what the item is.

Resources:

- a box
- some items from your language lesson hidden inside.

Steps:

1 Ask the class to listen carefully.
2 Describe one of the items inside the box by giving small clues to the children such as:

English	French	German
It's yellow.	Il est jaune.	Es ist gelb.
It's small.	Il est petit.	Es ist klein.
It's an animal.	C'est un animal.	Es ist ein Tier.
It's shy.	Il est timide.	Es ist schüchtern.

3 The children guess what the item is (*C'est un... / Es ist ein...*) and you take it out of the box only if they guess correctly!

LANGUAGE WHISPERS

A traditional favourite based on the 'Chinese Whispers' game which never fails to please! It is a good way to encourage children to remember, listen and pronounce words correctly in the foreign language.

- One or two children think of a word, phrase or famous person in France or Germany and whisper it to the child sitting next to them in the row or circle. In this way the word is passed around the class.
- The last person to receive the word tells the rest of the class whatever s/he has heard.
- The original version and the passed-around version are compared. Points could be awarded if the two versions are the same.

GUESS THE WORD

You need to write the first and last letters of a word that the children know where the class can see it. Can the children guess what the word is? An alternative to writing the letters is for you to mouth the word and for the children to guess what the word is. This is more fun to do than to describe – and the children may like to mouth their own words later. The focus is on looking at lips and mouths and reading the word on the face of the speaker. Thus facial expressions play a part here too, which is all part of learning a language.

UNSCRAMBLE THE WORD

This simple game is easy to organise and fun to do.

- Place a set of jumbled letters that make individual words on a board, flip chart or interactive whiteboard.
- Challenge the children (working in pairs, tables or teams) to unscramble the words: you could give them a set time by using a sand timer or a piece of French or German music.

JUMBLED WORDS

Display words from a practised sentence/question in the wrong order, for example, the beginning and ending of a fairy story (see Chapter 7, 'Exploring Stories') or a sentence you are rehearsing for an assembly perhaps (see Chapter 8, 'Showing the World'). Rearrange the words correctly with your class and then have a conversation using half the children to ask the question and the other half to say the expected answer.

PASS THE OBJECT

This is a game to use at the end of a unit where children have collected a number of nouns together (such as animal names, food and drink activities, classroom equipment) and preferably know some colours and how to make them agree. Before you start, work out together and write up prominently a few examples of objects to choose to support anxious children. All sit in a circle. One person begins by holding an imaginary object in their arms and saying *Dans mes bras j'ai...* and then uses a noun and an adjective to qualify what they are holding. For example a child might say *Dans mes bras j'ai un singe marron/ un crayon bleu/ une glace au chocolat*. This gives lots of scope. The next child takes the object appropriately (for example, licks an ice cream, catches a monkey etc.) and either repeats the same words to pass on, or changes them to something quite different such as *Dans mes bras j'ai un petit bébé*. Go round the circle and continue the game.

CLOSING THE CLASS AND SAYING GOODBYE

Here are some simple instructions your class will soon get used to understanding. They will quickly become part of the farewell routine if used regularly. Additional phrases are included in Appendix 3 as well.

English	French	German
Listen carefully!	Écoutez bien !	Hört gut zu!
Look at me!	Regardez-moi !	Schaut mich an!
Please shut the window!	Fermez la fenêtre !	Macht das Fenster bitte zu!
Stand up quietly!	Levez-vous doucement !	Steht ruhig auf!
Get into a line!	Mettez-vous en ligne !	Steht in einer Reihe!

These farewell exchanges you can use on a regular basis:

T = Teacher
C = Children

English	French	German
Goodbye everyone!	T: Au revoir tout le monde !	T: Auf Wiedersehen Kinder!
	C: Au revoir Madame X / Monsieur X	C: Auf Wiedersehen Herr X / Frau X!
See you tomorrow!	T: À demain !	T: Bis Morgen!
	C: À demain Madame / Monsieur !	C: Bis Morgen Herr X / Frau X!

A FAREWELL SONG

Singing goodbye at the end of the school day allows everyone to leave the classroom on an upbeat note! It is not difficult to fit lyrics around popular tunes that students already know, thereby consolidating the target language and having fun at the same time!

Example:

This farewell song can be sung to the tune of *Frère Jacques*.

French version	German version
Au revoir x 2	Auf Wiedersehen x 2
À demain x 2	Bis Morgen x 2
Nous allons à la maison x 2	Wir gehen nach Hause x 2
Dormez bien ! x 2	Schlaft gut! x 2

Resources: your voice!

Steps:

1 Children need to watch your face as you lead the group.
2 Display the words either on the board or on the wall of your classroom and take the song through line by line. Focus on pronunciation the first time you try it together.
3 The second time you sing the song, try adding some gestures such as waving goodbye and walking your fingers through the air as you sing about going home. When you sing about sleeping, place your two hands underneath your head which, in turn, is tilted to one side.

French and German Alphabets

French alphabet			
A	ah	**N**	en
B	bay	**O**	oh
C	say	**P**	pay
D	day	**Q**	ku
E	euh	**R**	air
F	eff	**S**	ess
G	jzhay (like j'ai)	**T**	tay
H	ash	**U**	oo
I	ee	**V**	vay
J	jzhee	**W**	doobler vay
K	ka	**X**	iks
L	ell	**Y**	ee grek
M	em	**Z**	zed

German alphabet

A	ah	N	en
B	bay	O	oh
C	tsay	P	pay
D	day	Q	ku
E	ay	R	air
F	eff	S	ess
G	gay	T	tay
H	ha	U	oo
I	ee	V	fow (like cow)
J	yot (like yacht)	W	vay
K	ka	X	iks
L	ell	Y	upsilon
M	em	Z	tset

Useful Classroom Language (plural familiar form)

English	French	German
Listen!	Écoutez !	Hört zu!
Look (at)!	Regardez !	Seht her!
Stand up!	Levez-vous !	Steht auf!
Sit down!	Asseyez-vous !	Setzt euch!
Calm down!	Calmez-vous !	Seid leise!
Repeat!	Répétez !	Wiederholt!
Write...	Écrivez...	Schreibt...
...in your books!	...dans les cahiers !	...in eure Bücher!
...on the board!	...au tableau !	...an die Tafel!
Find!	Cherchez !	Findet!
Get into a line!	Mettez-vous en ligne !	Steht in einer Reihe!
Guess!	Devinez !	Ratet!
Copy!	Copiez !	Kopiert!
Underline!	Soulignez !	Unterstreicht!
Work...	Travaillez...	Arbeitet...
...in groups!	...en groupe !	...in Gruppen!
...in pairs!	...à deux !	...zu zweit!
...in silence	...en silence !	...leise
...with a partner	...avec un partenaire !	...mit einem Partner

APPENDIX 3
Praise, Encouragement and Being Polite

English	French	German
Excellent!	Génial !	Super!
Well done!	Bien fait !	Gut gemacht!
Great!	Magnifique !	Toll!
Very good	Très bien !	Sehr gut!!
Good work!	Bon travail !	Gute Arbeit!
Please!	S'il vous plaît !	Bitte!
Thank you!	Merci !	Danke!
Slower!	Plus lent !	Langsamer!
Louder!	Plus fort !	Lauter!
Careful!	Attention !	Vorsicht!

Bibliography

Cambell, R. (1982) *Dear Zoo*. London: Abelard-Schuman.

Carle, E. (1969) *The Very Hungry Caterpillar*. London: Hamish Hamilton.

Carle, E. (2013) *Ours blanc, dis-moi....* New York: French and European Publications Inc.

Emberley, E. (2012) *Va-t'en, Grand Monstre vert*. Devon: Little Linguist.

Gravett, E. (2007) *Meerkat Mail*. London: Pan Macmillan.

Hedderwick, M. (1985) *Katie Morag and the Two Grandmothers*. London: Bodley Head.

McKee, D. (1989) *Elmer*. London: Anderson Press.

Martin, B. and Carle, E. (2001) *Ours brun, dis-moi....* New York: French and European Publications Inc.

Martin, Jr. B. and Carle, E. (1967) *Brown Bear, Brown Bear, What do you see?* New York: Holt Rinehart and Winston.

Rosen, M. (1989) *We're Going on a Bear Hunt*. London: Walker Books.

Sparrow, K. (2009) *Mega Manga: The Complete Reference to Drawing Manga*. Kent: Search Press Limited.

Watts, C., Forder, C. and Phillips, H. (2013) *Living Languages: An Integrated Approach to Teaching Foreign Languages in Primary Schools*, edited by Catherine Watts. Abingdon: Routledge.